SHOOT!

Shoot!

How to make a video film
to professional standards

Nigel McCrery

SIMON & SCHUSTER

LONDON·SYDNEY·NEW YORK·TOKYO·SINGAPORE·TORONTO

First published in Great Britain by
Simon & Schuster Ltd in 1993
A Paramount Communications Company

Simon & Schuster Ltd
West Garden Place
Kendal Street
London W2 2AQ

Simon & Schuster of Australia Pty Ltd
Sydney

A CIP catalogue record for this book is
available from the British Library
ISBN 0–671–71183–0

Typeset in 10/11.5 Sabon by
Florencetype Ltd, Kewstoke, Avon

Printed and bound in Great Britain by
The Bath Press, London and Bath

The author and publishers would like
to thank Jessops Cameras & Videos
for their expert assistance and loan
of equipment

This book is dedicated to the
BBC TAPS scheme of 1990/92:
Ben Fox, Ben Gale, Clara Glyn,
Bridget Caldwell,
Helen Hawkes, James Reed, Rajan Datar,
Laura Granditer, Sophie Manhan,
Susie Chapman, Pat Eastburn,
Katherine Edwards, Julia Hall,
Sue Hillman.

Contents

Preface

Television started as home movies. When John Logie Baird invented it in 1924 he could only transmit the outline of shapes, and even two years later when he first sent images of moving objects only friends and colleagues could see the results. Indeed when the BBC began the world's first high-definition public TV broadcasts in 1936 barely 30 people had the sets to watch it. If the British created television, the Japanese democratised it. Miniaturisation and mass-production of camera and video-tape technology has given millions of people the chance not just to watch TV but make it. Not surprisingly most of the programmes that result are amateur in the worst sense of the word – home video usually means jerky pictures taken without forethought and with little sense of continuity or composition, jump-cuts between long and dreary sequences, and truly dreadful sound. The camera usually moves more than the subject it is out to capture. If all you are seeking to achieve are archive pictures for the family of holidays and children growing up then that sort of wobbly-scope is fine.

If you want more, above all if you hope to make home video that people really want to watch, it really isn't hard to transform wobbly-scope to a passable imitation of professional TV. You do not need network broadcast budgets to use many of the best techniques – in fact usually all it takes is a readiness to learn from the experience of others and the patience to try things out before you put them into practice.

Think back to the problems confronting the BBC producers who had the task of starting a new genre. In their case, of course, since video-recording was unavailable, everything was live and every mistake would show to everyone's embarrassment or boredom. (This is more or less the problem you face, even with a camcorder, unless you have access to facilities for editing and dubbing.) So first they looked at what was done in radio and theatre but above all in the movies; they copied wholesale what had been developed over thirty years of cinema. Then they experimented with the remarkable new technology at their disposal – they put it through its paces to find out what it could do and what it couldn't. They tried different lighting, different lenses, different camera movements. And though they were adventurous they kept most of their experiments off air. The results, so far as they can be judged from film taken of these early broadcasts, cause those of us who follow these pioneers half a century later to be full of awe and humility. Quite simply they got it right.

Nigel McCrery sets out here some simple do's and dont's. Read the whole book and you will find almost everything you need to know about the art of making television amateur in the *best* sense of the word. Skim for what you need and you'll find lots of good advice. If you do nothing more than read this preface please, please, please at least (unless you have planned what you are doing) keep your camera still and let the subject that you're shooting do the moving!

Good reading, good shooting, good viewing.

Nick Ross

Introduction

Anyone can make a film. It really isn't that hard. For years people were using cine cameras to capture on film a vast variety of subjects. Most filmed important events in their own lives, their children growing up, parties or special occasions such as weddings, christenings or the village fête. Others still decided to capture more important events. They produced travel logs, early moving glimpses of times long past. Rounding the horn in a sailing ship, a royal visit, a trip to some exotic foreign part such as India or Africa. The archives are full of such historically important films, most made by amateur camera men with a desire to capture on film important bits of their own lives and to create a lasting memory for future generations to watch and enjoy. Even the royal family, appreciating film's historical importance, acquired one of the early cine cameras. There are a number of films showing Queen Victoria, Edward VII and their families enjoying themselves at one of their many family homes.

The major problem with cine film was that it was expensive, often came without sound, and you had to wait weeks before you saw the results of your efforts. Today things have changed dramatically. With the advent of the video camera, the ability to make a film has been made available to a far wider range of people. As the price of cameras is reduced, more second-hand cameras become available, and the ability to hire cameras becomes more widely spread, so people's capability to make a film grows.

What has been noticeable over the last few years is the degree of sophistication the camcorders have reached. All have sound, most have faders, instant replay, auto-focus and zoom lenses as well as a host of other devices to make your film more interesting and entertaining. The type of video tape being used in cameras is of a much higher standard, producing excellent picture quality. More recent, and I feel more important, is the advent of good quality editing equipment. The ability to dub a voice or music over your film, and to be able to move the pictures around losing little picture quality, has led to a revolution in programme making. It has enabled every amateur would-be film or documentary maker to make a film, of whatever length, and give it a professional feel. No less a body than the BBC were quick to see this. In programmes like *Video Diaries* and *Teenage Diaries* ordinary people are given video cameras and allowed to make their own film, with some astonishing results. It demonstrates that virtually untrained people are more than capable of making a fascinating film which often shows the side of a story that is rarely covered by professional film makers.

In this book I hope to demonstrate how each one of us can make a short film. I believe that the two key aspects of film making are firstly, to tell the story that you want to tell, as clearly and as professionally as you can and secondly, that the film should have an effect on its audience, whoever that audience happens to be. Only your skill as a film maker can do that.

What I hope to demonstrate is how to make that job easier, and give you some general ideas that might make your film more interesting, creative and more importantly, enjoyable to make and watch. I have also tried to keep it as simple as possible so that each person that reads it can get something from it.

I have based this book largely on the lessons I learned while training to work as part of a BBC production team. Some of you will doubtless disagree with some of the things I have said or know different techniques. I make no apology for this, these techniques have worked for me and countless others and I hope will also work for you. There are no right or wrong ways to make a programme or film, only different ways. So try out different techniques, practise as much as possible, and most of all enjoy it.

Nigel McCrery
May 1993

PART 1

Your Camera and Equipment

1

Cameras

When buying your first camcorder you will find there is a vast array to choose from, far too vast for inclusion in this book. However, there are a few points worth considering when making up your mind. Firstly, if you are considering purchasing a new camcorder then choose a reputable camera shop. There will normally be well-trained assistants on hand to advise you and help you select the camera that will best fit your needs. Also if you have any problems they should have a good after-sales and advice service. Secondly, it may be worth hiring a camera and discovering for yourself which features are the most useful before making your final selection. It is also worth considering buying second-hand; it will certainly cut down on your initial costs. Although you may not get a state-of-the-art camera, it should be fine to get you started and learn your craft. But if you do decide to go for a second-hand camera, be careful. Take someone with you who knows something about camcorders, to make sure that you are not sold a dud. If you have a friend who already has a video camera ask them for a demonstration and some advice based on their experiences. People are normally only too pleased to show off their skills. If you're really lucky, and they are a very good friend, they may even lend you a camera and allow you to make your own short film.

Camcorders will do most jobs. They come with a multitude of features: before buying think which features will be of most use to you.

Your next decision will be which type of camera to acquire. A palmcorder, a compact, or the traditional full-size camcorder. Your decision will depend largely upon your needs. As a general rule, if your requirements are simple and straightforward a palmcorder or a compact camcorder may be your best buy, although this does not mean they will be cheaper or less sophisticated. If you intend to try to make your own documentary or film a full-size camcorder with its greater range of facilities will be your best buy.

When you do finally decide to buy your first camera, you'll find prices do vary considerably, so shop around. But remember, the cheapest camcorder is not necessarily your best buy; as I outlined earlier there are other things to consider.

If your requirements are simple a palmcorder will be your best buy. They are light and easy to carry but not necessarily less sophisticated.

The Formats

One of your first considerations will be which format to choose. There are six currently on the market, the main difference between them being their size and recording quality.

Standard VHS

If you own a standard domestic video recorder then you will already be familiar with this format. It is by far the most popular and almost all the video films you buy and rent are produced in standard VHS. It has several advantages. Tapes can be played for up to 4 hours (or 8 if your camcorder has a long play facility), are cheap and readily available from most supermarkets and camera shops and picture quality is good. On the minus side the sound quality is only fair, and much will depend on the type of equipment you have. The tapes are very bulky and are normally used on split video recorders (camera and tape deck as separate units), which are heavy and quite awkward to carry around with you. Although there are now a number of all-in-one camcorders on the market, they are heavy, difficult to carry around and are all shoulder mounted. On the plus side the weight does help add to the stability of the camera and cut down on picture shake.

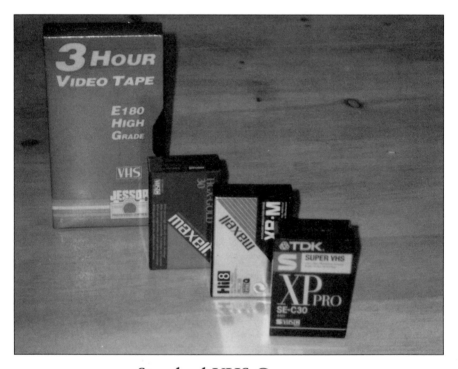

Standard VHS-C

There are a number of different formats on the market, the main difference between them being size and recording quality.

Much the same as above, but as the 'C' indicates it is designed for a lightweight compact camera. They are limited to between 30 and 45 minutes of playing time (at standard play time), although this can be doubled by using the long play (LP) facility on your camcorder (with a slight reduction in picture quality). They also

10

require a special adapter before you can replay them in your video recorder (normally supplied when you buy your camera).

There are two types of adapter to choose from:

1 Automatic adapter which converts your tape by using a small battery powered motor to stretch your tape to size. These can be quite expensive and I feel a little unnecessary.

2 Manual adapter which converts your tape by the use of a small lever attached to the adapter. These are cheaper (about half the price), easy to use and ideal for the job.

Super-VHS and Super VHS-C

This format will provide you with a greatly improved picture quality. Some TV stations already supply S-VHS equipment to their news crews. Sound quality however is only fair. It is also worth remembering that your standard VHS cassette recorder will not play the super-VHS format. So you will either have to buy a video cassette deck that will take the super-VHS format, or convert your tape to standard VHS before watching it. This does however seem to defeat the object of having a super-VHS camcorder in the first place. Both the cameras and the tapes are more expensive and there is a limited range of camcorders to choose from.

Video 8

Video 8 is totally different. Instead of the standard 1½-inch tape video 8 uses an 8mm tape. Although this makes the tape the smallest on the market it still manages to have a maximum running time of 90 minutes (one and a half hours in long play). You can therefore have the convenience of a long-playing tape without the problems of having a heavy and bulky standard VHS camera. Both sound and picture quality are good. However there are few video recorders that will re-play them, mainly because there are few pre-recorded tapes to buy or rent at the moment. (This situation is slowly improving.) This means you will have to play your tape directly into the television set, or re-record from the original tape on to a standard VHS format. By doing so however you will lose picture quality. Video 8 is considered, by many, to be the format of the future.

High 8

High 8 offers a very high standard of picture quality (higher than standard 8mm) and produces a very sharp image. This format is popular with professional television crews, especially when it comes to secret or difficult filming trips. The tapes have a long play time, are small and light and both picture and sound quality is excellent. Because of their size they are also easy to smuggle out should the need arise. Although camcorders with this format were initially very expensive they are beginning to come down in price.

Camcorder Features

When choosing your camera your two priorities have to be the quality of the pictures and the sound. Once that is decided, you will find yourself overwhelmed by the amount of different options video cameras have to offer. Before deciding what extras you need, consider what kind of film or programme you want to make and which extras the camera has to offer will best help you achieve your objectives. These are a few options you might like to consider:

Camera Weight

Remember you may have to carry your camera for miles, so the lighter the better. (Failing that convince the kids or your partner what a great honour it is to be allowed to carry the camera!) However, it is also worth remembering that you will get less camera shake on weightier cameras so it may be worth the effort.

Camera equipment can be heavy so take someone strong with you.

Electronic Viewfinder Display

This will display all the information you need directly into the camcorder's viewfinder.

Auto Mode

Automatically controls exposure and white balance and helps eliminate many basic mistakes. All you have to do is aim the camera and shoot.

Shutter Modes

Provides a choice of shutter speeds between 1/50 and 1/10,000, allowing you to record fast-action sequences clearly and effectively.

Character Generator (Built in)

This allows you to put titles onto your film and gives the film a more professional look, as well as helping you to remember who's who (which can be very embarrassing if you get it wrong).

Audio Frequency Modulation (or AFM)

This provides first-class stereo sound if you feel you need it.

Time Function

This provides you with an interval timer so that you can film flowers opening and closing, for example, or any other very slow moving event.

Auto-Faders

Enables you to fade both vision and sound while you are recording, providing more interesting editing points and tricks.

Record-Review/Picture Search

Very good for a quick replay of a shot, especially when you are on location; saves having to go back later if you suddenly discover you have made a mistake.

Time-Code Generation Facilities

This will provide frame-accurate editing. Speeds up and makes editing your programme far easier.

Auto Date and Time

This will insert the time and date you took your film on to your tape.

Still Frame

Will help you to start each new shot at the correct place on your tape. Good for editing in camera and getting shots the right length and in the right order.

Power Zoom
Gives you fingertip control of zooms, from telephoto to wide angle shots.

Low Light
Allows you to film in lower light than usual. Any model capable of working at a light level of 10 lux or less will enable you to film inside without the need for additional lighting (although picture quality will be poor).

DC Light
The light mounted on the front of your camcorder. This makes it easier to film inside at children's parties, for example, where using fixed lighting is difficult.

Sound Extension Socket
Used for extension leads for additional microphones. This is a very useful way of improving the quality of your sound recording.

Earpiece Socket
Vital if you want to monitor the sound going into the tape.

Wind-Noise Filter Switch
Helps reduce wind noise through the microphone which can prove very annoying (a wind bag placed over the video microphone made of felt or some similar material will also do the job).

Back-Light Button (Manual iris control)
Opens up the lens aperture in order to give the foreground subject the correct exposure (stops the subject you are filming becoming black when shot against a bright background).

15

Additional (Add-on) Lenses

By using add-on lenses you can expand the camcorder's field of vision. The wide-angle lens will allow you to include items that would otherwise have been on the edge of your picture and the telephoto lens will bring the object of your attention even closer.

Add-on lenses can expand your field of vision, giving you wider angles or increasing the power of your telephoto lens.

Understanding Your Camera

Once you have your new camcorder, make sure you read the instructions carefully and become totally conversant with it. Take your time discovering how to use the different options, then start filming. Practise as much as possible, experiment, learn from your mistakes. It doesn't matter how many errors you make, you can always tape over them later.

At A Glance

1   When purchasing your camera go for picture and sound quality first.

2   Consider carefully which format best suits your needs.

3   Do not become overwhelmed by the amount of gadgets that come with the cameras. Consider which options suit you best and stick to them.

4   Read your instructions carefully and get to know your camera well before you start to make your film or programme.

5   Start to use it.

2

Sound

New film makers often neglect sound, concentrating instead on the pictures. As will soon be discovered however, the sound is every bit as important, and should, therefore, like your pictures, be as natural and creative as possible.

Through sound you are able to convey to your audience precise information. A time, a date or a location. More importantly, sound is able to create mood and atmosphere, add realism and intensify the action. To fully appreciate its importance, the next time you watch an action-packed video film, first watch it with sound and then without. You will find that the pictures, without the accompanying sound, become dead and less interesting. Even films like *Psycho* and *Jaws* would not have had the same impact without the creative use of sound.

You will soon notice that different locations and events have their own particular and distinct sounds. Next time you are out stop for a moment and listen: observe how the noises made in the high street with its cars, buses, busy shoppers and street traders will be different from those made in the local park. Even sounds that you would imagine to be similar are often quite different. For instance, the sounds made by a crowd at a football match are very different from the sounds made at, say, a rugby or cricket match, and those sounds will again be different from the noises made by a crowd at a demonstration. When filming in these locations make sure you recreate the various sounds as accurately as possible, or you may well lose the aura you are trying to recreate.

You can make a sequence more interesting, amusing or fill it with foreboding or menace by choosing the right piece of music or sound effect. Therefore to help make your programme more exciting, collect and record these sounds carefully and learn to use them to their best possible effect. You can either recreate the sound effects yourself or with the help of friends, or failing that, buy any one of a number of sound-effect tapes and discs that are on the market. It is also worth making a note of any piece of music that you feel might help add interest to your programme.

Recording Your Sound

Recording the sound, like making the rest of your film or programme, becomes a matter of making the right decisions from the start. Which mike are you going to use? Should you use a radio mike, boom or clip mike? How close to your subject should you be? The decisions you make will be vital and affect the way your film is finally presented. It is important therefore that the decisions you make are the right ones.

All video cameras have microphones attached. However, these are not generally of the best quality, and can present a multitude of problems. The fixed-camera microphones are poor at recording speech, especially when the subject is more than a few metres away, and few models have any provision for manual control of sound. They also pick up unwanted sounds, like passing traffic, aircraft engines and the wind, which can ruin a shot or sequence. Therefore, to get the best sound quality possible, use a separate microphone. There are a number to choose from, several of which

19

are designed to do a different job. They fall into two main categories:

1 Omnidirectional, which pick up sound equally in every direction and are good for general atmosphere sounds. However, they are also liable to pick up unwanted noises like the sound of traffic.

Although all video cameras have built-in mikes, to get the best sound quality use a separate one. There is a vast array to choose from.

2 Unidirectional, which pick up sound only in the direction in which the microphone is pointed. With this type of microphone it is important to be accurate when directing your microphone at your subject, otherwise you are still likely to pick up unwanted noises.

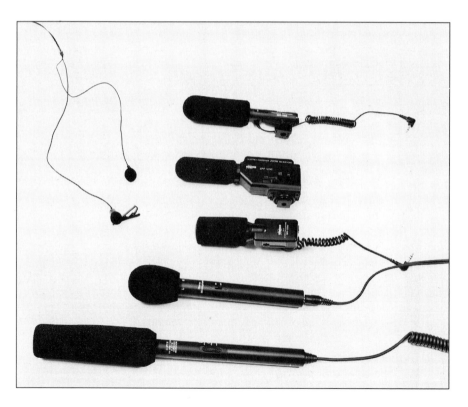

When acquiring your microphone try to obtain the best quality you can afford. Electret models use a polarised condenser instead of a crystal (which the cheaper models use, and which are not very good for sound reproduction on video). Electret microphones will give you a good, clear sound. They are reasonably priced, and excellent for general use (although they do require batteries). You could also consider a Dynamic microphone. The sound quality is excellent, and they are especially good when it comes to recording music.

Below is a selection of the microphones you might like to consider.

Stick Microphone
This can either be held in your hand or mounted on a stand. It can be used as either a uni- or omnidirectional microphone and is very versatile, being especially useful for street interviews and general sound.

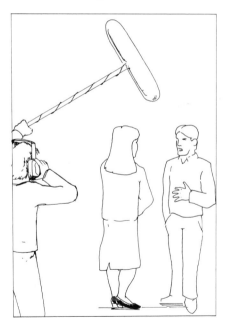

By mounting your microphone on a boom you are able to position your mike over the heads of a crowd and pick out individual speakers.

21

Boom Microphone

This is a unidirectional microphone mounted on a boom. It enables you to position the mike over the heads of a crowd and pick out an individual speaker. Although it works very well, it can be difficult to use, and requires practice. When using a boom microphone obviously you will find a sound assistant essential.

Gun Microphone

A super-directional microphone which is aimed at an individual sound source or speaker. It is used rather like an acoustic equivalent of the telephoto lens. Marvellous for eliminating unwanted noise, it is used mostly for outdoor recording. Once again fairly difficult to use, and it will take practice. A sound assistant will normally be required.

Clip Microphone

This is a miniature microphone which clips onto a subject's clothes. It can be positioned so that it is invisible in shot. In certain situations however it doesn't really matter if it is visible; in fact it can often give your film a

Clip microphones should eliminate most background sounds but they do have a tendency to pick up noises made by your subject's clothes, so keep them still.

22

certain air of professionalism if the mike can be seen. If you position it within a few inches of the speakers lips, it should eliminate nearly all other background noise and produce a strong signal from your subject. It is of little use however when trying to record speech from a group of people or crowd. A clip microphone is available as a cable-connection, which can limit movement, or as a radio mike. The major problem with it is that it has a tendency to pick up the noise made by a subject's clothing if he or she moves around too much, so beware.

Hand Microphone

A hand-held microphone gives you the freedom to move around. However, it's worth taking some time rehearsing with it before using it in front of camera. With practice it will be an asset to you.

Radio Microphone

This gives you a greater freedom of movement: the tiny transmitter can be hidden in your back pocket and allows you to move wherever you want (within the range of the transmitter) without a lead following you

Radio mikes slip into your back pocket easily and give you a greater freedom of movement.

everywhere. You can also use a radio mike to provide some spectacular sequences in which, although you can see a person in a long shot, you can hear them close-up. Good examples of this are: someone flying a hand glider or standing on a distant hillside.

Headphones

Although personal stereo headphones and earpieces are better than nothing, they do allow undesirable noises to seep in. So try to get hold of a good set of closed-back hi-fi cans. They are expensive, but are an investment and well worth the extra money. A good set of cans will quickly pick up any unwanted sounds and allow you to adjust the position of your mike to avoid them.

Audio Mixers

Under certain circumstances you will need to use a number of mikes, and you will therefore have to combine their signals. To do this effectively you will need an audio mixer. Either (if you are technically minded) build one yourself, or get one from your local video or electrical stockist (they are also useful as a volume control). Acquire one that has built-in level meters, enabling you to balance up all the microphones you are using with far more accuracy than just listening on a set of headphones. Do check the sound levels before beginning a recording. To do this, ask your subject or subjects to say a few words in turn into the microphone (it doesn't matter what they say), and then adjust your mixer levels accordingly. You will also find a tone control useful. The most sophisticated form of this is a graphic equaliser, which should remove most unwanted sounds from your recording.

Handling

The way you handle your microphone is as important as the type of microphone you buy. With a hand-held microphone make sure you hold it firmly and still, cutting down on handling noises. Hold it at about chest height and about 12 inches away from the subject. Do not speak directly into the microphone but aim instead at a point just above it. This should reduce popping, hissing and noises made by breathing. Tilt the microphone towards the interviewee and always have sufficient cable (if you have any) if you are moving about in shot. Speak at a constant level and a little slower than normal, but try to keep it natural. If you do make a mistake you can always record it again. Reduce the strain of an interview by making yourself and your interviewee as comfortable as possible. Before recording, it's always worth making a few simple sound checks by moving the microphone around and making some test recordings; it can save you a great deal of time in the long run.

Having microphones and their shadows in shot can be a problem. There are certain rules however that should help you overcome these difficulties. Hand-held microphones, microphones mounted on tables, and clip mikes attached to clothing are acceptable in shot, other microphones are not. Seeing a microphone fall into shot during a TV play can ruin even the most moving of sequences, drawing the viewer's concentration away from the actors and making the whole scene slightly ridiculous. Rehearse for a few moments before setting up your shot, giving yourself enough time to work out the best position for your microphone. This should help you to avoid getting either your microphone, or its shadow, in shot before you start filming. If you think this may have happened, then play the sequence back and check. It's better to do a re-run than to produce a sloppy sequence.

The location for your film or interview can be of great importance. It is one of the few things that is, for the most part, under your control. When filming outside the most common problem you will face will be the wind. Even a slight breeze can sound like a gale to an unprotected microphone. To help combat this problem

25

it is a good idea to either buy or make yourself an acoustic foam wind gag to cover your microphone. Although this will cut down the noise it will not eliminate it completely so try shielding the microphone with your body or get behind some form of cover.

Unwanted noises can be another problem, trains, planes, cars and children screaming being the most popular. You can either wait for the unwanted noise to move away, bribe them or try pointing the mike in the other direction. Failing those however try to find a quieter location with a minimum of unwanted noises. (Your location check should have sorted this out before you started shooting – see chapter 8). Recording indoors can also create problems. Sound will bounce off any flat, unabsorbent surface, such as walls, ceilings, flat-topped tables or uncurtained windows. So the more soft furnishings there are around, such as carpets and

Unwanted noises can be a serious problem, so choose your location carefully.

26

curtains, the less your sound will be reflected and the better your reproduction will be.

After shooting your scene or sequence it is a good idea to get a wild or buzz track – that is, to get some background or atmosphere sounds from your location. These can be edited onto your tape later and cover any awkward gaps in the synchronised sound track. Seagulls, the sound of the wind through the trees, the noise of a boat's engine: can all be helpful later. Remember, even the quietest location, such as a church or museum, can have its own distinct sounds.

Finally (as I hope has become clear) it is a good idea to use a sound assistant. Many of the things you have to do will be much harder without one. He or she can not only monitor sound levels for you but can also make sure that the microphone is in the correct position to obtain the best sound quality possible. In my experience they are also very good at telling people to clear off (quietly)!

A sound assistant is invaluable. He or she can monitor the sound and make sure the mikes are in the right position.

27

At A Glance

1 Remember there are copyright restrictions on the use of music even for private viewings, which must be cleared. But there are specially cleared themes you can obtain for use with your film.

2 Collect as many sound effects as you can, you never know when they are going to come in handy. A barking dog, church bells, creaking door etc. may all be useful. You could even try to create your own with coconut shells, combs, boxes of gravel, sheets of cardboard. Use your friends to recreate certain crowd noises. Create your own music using a synthesiser or electronic organ.

3 When interviewing try to select a quiet location and if possible recce the place first to try to spot any possible problems.

4 Rehearse before you start recording, to allow you to check your sound levels and correct any problems.

5 If you do have problems do it again until you are satisfied that it is right.

6 Creating sound is one of the most entertaining parts of making a film so enjoy it and have fun.

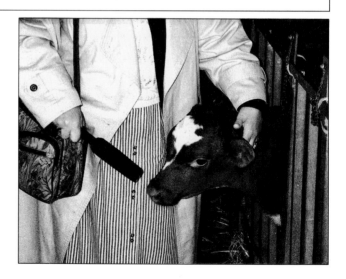

Collecting your own sound effects can be a great deal of fun.

28

3

Lighting

Although lighting your scene properly is vital if you are going to produce good quality pictures, it can be more important even than that. Used effectively, lighting can make your subject appear more attractive, or sinister, add depth to a scene or give it a more natural feel. More importantly, it can establish atmosphere and mood, helping to appeal to the emotions of your audience.

Natural Light

When filming outside in fine sunny conditions, be aware of the sun's position at all times. If you shoot with the sun directly behind your subject he is likely to be silhouetted and appear dark on screen. Even if you increase your exposure via the camcorder's back-light button, it will make little difference. Your subject's face will still appear flat and unattractive.

On the other hand, if you shoot with the sun behind you, your subject will probably be too severely lit. Also, by being forced to look towards the sun your subject is likely to squint and screw their faces up.

It is far easier to position your subject so that the sun is either directly above them or slightly to one side, although even then you can have problems. Illuminating your subject from the side will only light

29

If you shoot with the sun directly behind your subject, he is likely to be silhouetted and appear dark on screen.

one side of your subject and leave the other dark and in shadow. Lighting from above can produce deep shadows below your subject's nose (the bigger the nose the bigger the problem, so avoid people with big noses) or the inside of eye sockets. Therefore, try to keep your light as even as possible. The best way to do this is to have two sources of light. Your main source of light illuminating one side of your subject, and a secondary, less powerful source illuminating any unwanted shadows on the opposite side. Your main source of light, in

30

this case the sun, is called the key light and your secondary source the fill light.

Reflectors

When shooting outside you can use the sun as both your key and fill lights. To achieve this you will need a reflector. Reflectors normally come in silver, gold and white. They are available from most good camera shops, are inexpensive and an important addition to your equipment. Silver reflectors tend to produce a cool harsh light, whereas gold tends to give a sort of warm glow. White reflectors are excellent for general use and can be made quite easily from a piece of white card. If

When shooting outside it's best to use the sun as both your key and fill lights. To do this you will need a reflector.

31

you become really stuck you can convert almost any-thing with a white surface (I've even used a piece of newspaper). Most of the reflectors you can purchase will have silver on one side and gold on the other, so you will have a choice and it's up to you which side is best for a particular shot. Reflectors do however have their limitations and while fine for static interviews they are difficult to use for moving shots.

Additional Lighting

Lights come in a bewildering assortment of shapes, sizes and prices. When selecting which light or combination of lights you need there are a number of points worth considering.

Basically there are four types of lights:

1 Mains-powered lights.

2 Clip-on accessory lights. Normally they will be sup-plied with the machine and will draw their power from the camcorder's own battery pack.

3 Those powered by their own built-in NiCad battery pack.

4 Ones which are run from an external lead-acid bat-tery pack.

One of your main considerations when selecting your lights must be their power output. This is normally quoted in watts, and the higher the better. A warning however: if you are using batteries, remember, the higher the wattage, the more power your light will use, and this will reduce your running time. The best way to cope with this problem is to work out a time-power ratio and stick to it. That way you shouldn't find your-self half way through a shoot when the power to your lights runs out. It's also a good idea to have a fully charged spare battery with you (just in case).

Types of Light

Self Powered

Self powered lights, although light and easy to carry, have serious limitations. They have a low output and short running times (between 10 and 20 minutes) so ensure you have your time-power ratio handy and watch the clock.

Shoulder-Slung

Shoulder-slung battery-powered lights are fairly power-ful, with an output of about 100 watts, and run for about half an hour. On the negative side they are very heavy, and lead-acid batteries can take over half a day to recharge so you may need several (which can be expensive).

Hand-held lights are best used for lighting small groups of people. They work off shoulder-slung 12 volt batteries. Used as the only source of light however they will create a flat effect.

Mains Powered

Mains powered lights are the most powerful and will run for as long as you like. However, your lights must remain within reach of a mains socket, which can limit your mobility. So make sure there are plenty of power points at your location and that you have a good length of extension cable. It is also worth remembering that if you have to use a lot of extension cables, make sure they are covered with rubber matting or similar. The last thing you want is people tripping over the cables and injuring themselves, or smashing the equipment.

Converting Your Lighting

Despite the fact that many cameras are now able to work in less than 10 lux of light (equivalent of candle light) picture quality suffers. You will find the pictures becomes grainy and crude, the colours become weaker and look washed out. Therefore there are going to be many occasions when you will require additional lighting to improve your pictures. For the best picture quality you will require around 900 lux of light, (remembering that the average room's lighting is between 100 and 300 lux). This does not mean that you will have to rush out and buy specialist lighting. First try to make the best use of your available lighting. Surprisingly, there's a lot of it. You can often produce as much illumination as you need by adapting your domestic lighting. For instance, if you are filming in your sitting room and want to improve your general lighting, take the shades off your standard and over-head lamps and increase the wattage in the bulbs. A word of warning however: be careful not to overload your lights. If you want to improve lighting in a partic-ular area again try to use available lighting. Move the standard and table lights to their best advantage, increase the power of the bulbs (again within the limits of safety), and try using a domestic spot lamp. If how-ever you are not happy with this arrangement you can purchase a wide variety of lamps that will help.

34

Additional Lighting

Fixed-Camera Lights

Several cameras are now equipped with portable video lights which either come already fixed to the camera or can be attached later. These lights normally run on low-wattage quartz bulbs of between 10 and 25 watts which produce a hard, concentrated light best used for close-in shots or as a fill light for back-lit subjects. Although easy to use they can be a tremendous drain on the camcorder's batteries and reduce your shooting time.

Try to make the best use of your available lighting. This can work as well as professional lighting.

35

Fixed camcorder lights produce a hard, concentrated beam of light and are best for close-up work.

Hand-Held Quartz Lamp

Quartz lamps normally run off a 75 to 250 watt bulb. These are hand held and powered by a shoulder-slung 12 volt battery. They are very good for lighting small groups of people. A single lamp used as the only source of light, whether fixed to the camera or hand held can produce unwanted background shadows as well as make your subject(s) look flat and uninteresting. To help overcome this try bouncing or reflecting the light off your walls or ceilings; this can produce a much more natural effect.

Floodlights

There are quite a number of floodlights on the market, with lamp wattage ranging between 500 and 1000 watts. They are all fitted with safety glass and this produces some diffusion of the light although the more expensive lamps also have mountings for either additional diffuser or filters for a greater range of effects. Many come with sets of hinged flaps, known as barn doors, which are used to direct the beam. If you are using lights with barn doors be careful – the hinged flaps do get very hot. Most lamps are available either as a wide-beam unit, which is good for general lighting, or as spot-lamps which are able to concentrate their beam. A variable-focus lamp is also worth considering as it can be used for both purposes.

Mixed Lighting

Mixed lighting can cause problems. Because each source of light emits light of a different colour temperature, and therefore a different colour, mixing natural and artificial light can change the colour balance of your picture. Mixed lighting can also play havoc with your white balance. However the correct filters will normally correct any imbalance.

Bouncing Light

Bouncing light is an important technique which is worth spending time learning. The idea is to bounce

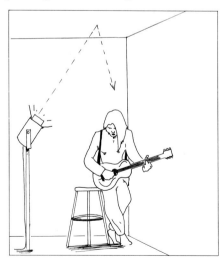

Bouncing light off reflective surfaces produces a diffused, low-contrast light ideal for video. But beware coloured walls.

your light off a reflective surface such as a wall, low ceiling or reflector onto your subject. Although bouncing light will reduce the illumination produced by your lamp, it does produce a diffused, low-contrast lighting ideal for video. Avoid strongly coloured walls; they tend to cast their own colour on your subject, often with hilarious or embarrassing results.

Lighting Positions

The next stage is to learn how to use your lights correctly. The basic lighting arrangement is known as the three-lamp system. The first lamp is used as a back light. This light creates a halo of light from behind

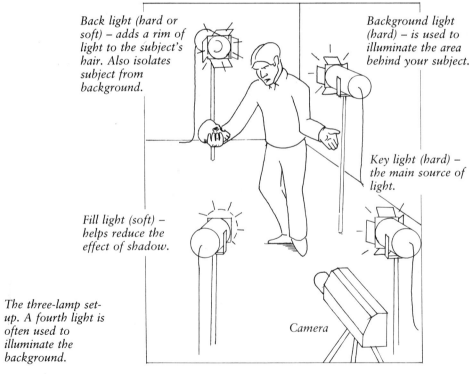

Back light (hard or soft) – adds a rim of light to the subject's hair. Also isolates subject from background.

Background light (hard) – is used to illuminate the area behind your subject.

Key light (hard) – the main source of light.

Fill light (soft) – helps reduce the effect of shadow.

The three-lamp set-up. A fourth light is often used to illuminate the background.

Camera

which separates the subject from the background. Normally a spot light is used for this purpose because it produces a concentrated beam which can be directed at a particular area. The key light is next. This light establishes the general level of exposure but should be set far enough back to avoid a harsh appearance. Position it to provide front light but at an angle to your subject and point the lamp downwards at approximately 45 degrees to the horizontal. The third light is the fill light. This light is positioned on the opposite side of the camera to the key light. It is normally fitted with an additional diffuser so as to soften the appearance of the subject and reduce the depth of the shadows. Position it so that it gives about half the lighting intensity of the key light. A fourth lamp may be used to light the background separately and to neutralise any shadows cast by the fill and key lights. Background light should always be lower than that of the foreground to give the scene depth and highlight your subject.

Experiment

Different lighting styles create different moods. High-key lights create a general feeling of brightness, while low-key lighting can be used to establish an air of mystery, drama and tension. Dramatic lighting can emphasise a certain portrayal. Lighting from beneath can distort facial features, making your subject look sinister and menacing. (While standing in front of a mirror in a darkened room try shining a torch from your chin upwards so it shines across your face. You will see what I mean.) Lighting from above can initiate a sombre, claustrophobic air; defuse lighting can make the scene more romantic. Take your time with the lights when establishing your scene, wait until you feel that the lights are creating the atmosphere you want before you start shooting.

At A Glance

1   Practise and look. It is the only way to improve your lighting judgement. Try using a portable monitor or miniature TV to help you determine both lighting and colour.

2   Always put safety first. Beware of hot lamps or barn doors. Make sure that tripod stands are secure and are not likely to be accidentally upset.

3   If possible use a separate mains socket for each lamp unit. Do not overload your lighting system and cover any cables covering the floor.

4   Use natural lighting wherever possible.

5   Check your shots to see if the lighting you have used works for that particular sequence or scene. If not, do it again.

6   Don't be afraid to use reflectors to balance the light on your subject.

7   If you are using additional lighting check that your batteries are fully charged or that you have spare sets.

8   Beware mixed lighting – it can change the colour balance on your picture.

4

Using and Abusing

Hand Held

Lightweight cameras are designed to be hand held. Although there will be some camera shake (even the professionals can't avoid that) they have enormous advantages for the user. Because you are able to keep them close to hand you can pick up the action quickly and spontaneously. It is easy to follow the action, you can vary your shots, and shooting from awkward and inconvenient places presents less of a problem. However hand-held filming does require time and practice to perfect. So get to know your camera and equipment until its use becomes second nature to you.

When using your camera try to make your body imitate a tripod. Stand with your feet slightly apart distributing your weight as evenly as possible. Place your right hand through the hand grip strap. Grip the camera firmly with both hands (remember, the lighter the camera the tighter your grip). Position your right thumb over the record button. Press the camera tightly against your face and keep your elbows tightly tucked in to your sides and relax. Use your other hand to help steady the camera and to operate the focus or zoom. If you have access to a shoulder support or camera brace then use it. It will certainly help reduce camera shake. Try using any available props like chairs, walls, the top

To avoid camera shake imitate a tripod: spread your weight evenly throughout your body.

of your car, or even your friend's back or shoulder; they will all help steady your shot. Camera shake is at its worst when you are using your zoom lens to film a static subject. To overcome this, use a wide-angle lens and move closer to your subject. This will achieve better results and eliminate any wobbly zooms. If you have to move to follow your subject then turn from the waist at half natural speed, making your movements rhythmical and deliberate, not jerky. Adopt a camera position that will allow you to cover the action without having to move too much. The more you practise the more your technique will improve.

Tripods and Stands

The Tripod

No matter how expert you become at hand holding your camera, it is only with a tripod that you will achieve absolute steadiness. Its adjustable legs allow you to film in both even and uneven terrain. It supports your camcorder and lets you take rock-steady shots and get the best results from your zoom or telephoto lens. Pans and tilts become smoother and more graceful and you are able to record time lapses, animation, landscapes and wildlife. Generally, your film will take on a more professional appearance. A versatile and good quality tripod is not an option, it is an essential.

When acquiring your tripod make sure it is stable (on any sort of ground), flexible (able to extend or splay its legs) and with a good tripod head, allowing the camera to be pivoted smoothly in all directions using the pan handle. The best head for your video tripod is a fluid one. Although expensive it is invaluable if you want

Make use of any available prop as support: the top of a car provides a convenient camera rest.

43

good quality pictures. Several tripods come with built-in spirit levels which are excellent for ensuring your shots are level. Also make sure you have a decent sized pan handle, making it easier to take steady panning shots; many professional camera men will have pan handles that are at least 2 feet long.

The tripod will make your shots smoother and the action easier to follow and will keep your camera level during pans and tilts. It is likewise essential when shooting lengthy events or interviews. It is also useful to be able to vary the height of the shots from your tri-

A good tripod is one of the most invaluable 'extras' you can buy.

pod, making your film more interesting. The two main disadvantages are that they are heavy to carry, and take time to set up, having a dampening effect on spontaneity. However the disadvantages are heavily outweighed by the advantages. In the end it comes down to what do you want most, an easy life or a good film.

When using your tripod make sure that it's securely placed to avoid accidents. Stand firmly between its legs, adjusting them to give you a comfortable operating position during movement. Hold the pan handle firmly with one hand, keeping your elbow well into your side. Use the other hand to operate the controls on the camera.

You can also use your tripod to create special effects. Set up a static scene – an empty sitting room will do (so long as there is nothing moving in the room). Set up your camera and tripod and then lock your tripod off (so the camera is unable to move). After shooting a few seconds of film of your empty sitting room, pause. Then get someone to move into shot and start filming again; it will look like they appeared as if by magic. By using a variety of combinations of this technique you can achieve remarkable effects.

When you buy your tripod try it out first. Get it set up in the shop. Test the pan and tilt heads for ease of movement. See how heavy it is – remember it's you who will have to carry it. See how strong and stable it is and how far the legs extend. Although there are cheap tripods on the market, if you spend less than £40 on one you could be asking for trouble. It is one of the accessories worth spending a bit of money on, because it will make so much difference to your filming.

Monopod

If you are unable to manage the cost, weight or bulk of a tripod then a monopod may be the obvious solution. It doesn't offer the same degree of lateral stability that a tripod does, relying very much on a steady hand, but does however offer vertical stability, seating the cam-

A monopod, although it doesn't offer the same degree of lateral stability as a tripod, does provide vertical stability. It is also lighter and cheaper.

corder firmly on the ground or another support and stopping any up and down movements.

Universal Pod/Brace

Occasionally you will find that you need to keep your camcorder steady for long periods of time, but it isn't practical to use either a tripod or monopod. The answer may be a universal pod or camcord brace. These will help to keep your camera steady, while at the same time giving you the flexibility to move around. They normally consist of a shoulder or chest stock with an adjustable strap which can go around either the shoulder or neck. The shaft can normally be extended and locked to

46

To keep your camcorder steady for a long period of time a pod brace may be the answer.

suit various sizes of camera and for that matter camera operators. Once you have finished filming, it folds away to take up very little space in your gadget bag.

The Car Mount

Shooting from a car is almost impossible without some form of camcord support. Car supports connect to the camcorder and clamp firmly to the door assembly of the car, giving you shake-free pictures, provided that you can find a pot-free road.

The Steadicam

The Steadicam is a clever stabilising system which is specially weighted to suspend the camera in 'zero gravity'. It is an American invention which has revolutionised professional film and television making over the last few years. The Steadicam is ideal for restricting the up and down movement while filming on the move. Although good, the Steadicam has its limitations and is best suited for work with wide lenses. Tight lenses produce a drifting effect.

47

Keeping Dry

Rain can ruin many a day's filming and can be one of the greatest natural menaces a film maker can face. Assuming you don't have a water-resistant camcorder (and there are several on the market), you are going to have to devise ways of protecting your camera from the wet. A strong plastic bag cut to shape may be enough. On the other hand a number of manufacturers offer rather smarter variations. Manufactured rain bags are certainly of good quality and do a good job but they can be very expensive, ranging between £40 and £200. With care (and a bit of copying) it's probably as easy to make your own.

At A Glance

1   When hand holding your camera make your body imitate a tripod, with your feet slightly apart, distributing your weight evenly and holding your camera firmly.

2   Use any available props like a chair, a wall or the top of your car to help steady your shot.

3   When following a moving subject with your camera, turn your body from the waist. Turn at about half your natural speed.

4   Wherever possible use a tripod. It is the only real method of keeping your shots absolutely steady.

5   Try other kinds of support such as a monopod or a universal pod and brace.

6   Failing all else there are now cameras on the market with anti-shake facilities.

7   Make your own wet weather bag – it's more fun and a lot cheaper than buying one.

5

The Shots

Films are, in essence, just a series of separate pictures taken from different angles and distances to form a sequence. In all professional television and film work, these pictures are given a standard description so that the camera operator knows exactly which shots are needed for the sequence. To make it easier to write down when organising your script the name of each shot is abbreviated. You will also soon discover that each shot will have a particular emotional impact on your audience, a fact worth considering when selecting your shots. Notice how a television news reader is never shown in more detail than a close-up. A big or extreme close-up shot would imply an intimacy that would be inappropriate, whereas a person speaking in a long shot would appear distant and isolated. These are all tricks worth learning when embarking on your film.

The main shot sizes used are (with their abbreviations):

Wide Shot (WS)

Long Shot (LS)

Medium Shot (MS)

Medium Close-up (MCU)

Close-up (CU)

I have outlined below the way some of the shots are used. I have also added some additional shots not mentioned above, but which you may find both interesting and helpful. Although these pointers can be used as a general guide, try to vary your shots as much as possible, and don't allow yourself to become restricted by the idea that certain shots should only be used for certain occasions. Experiment as much as possible. This way you will learn quickly and make far more interesting film.

Wide Shot (WS)
Normally introduced at the beginning of your sequence to establish the scene. The shot can be either static or moving, so long as it reveals the overall picture.

Long Shot (LS)
Although this will give you a wide establishing view it will also direct the attention of your audience to the

Very long shot

50

subject by isolating it from any distracting backdrop. *Long shot*
When the term is used in relation to a figure the camera can be a matter of yards or even feet away. For the
shot to be considered a long shot the subject should
take up half to two-thirds of the height of the picture.
A longer shot, where the subject appears small on the
horizon, is referred to as an extreme long shot (ELS).

Medium Shot (MS)

When filming a figure the medium shot (MS) should
cover an area from just below your subject's waist to
just above his head. It is the ideal opening shot for interviews or other scenes containing dialogue. Do not hold
the shot for too long however as it quickly becomes boring. Where two characters are seen together the shot is
referred to as a two shot. Shots taken between long
shots and medium shots are called medium long shots
(MLS).

51

Medium shot

Medium Close-up (MCU)

This shot cuts just below the armpits and is close enough to show the detail on your subject's face without being so close that it intrudes. This is the standard interview shot. It is also a good shot to cut to from the medium shot when that shot becomes tiresome.

Close-up (CU)

One of the most valuable video shots, it shows significant details of facial expressions. The close-up includes the whole of the head and shoulders of a person. Shots where only the head can be seen are known as the big close-ups. Close-ups are frequently used to show how people respond to each other, and for talking heads. You can also use this shot to give dramatic emphasis to an object or situation. The front of a car before it impacts against its victim, for example.

52

Developing Your Sequence

When developing your sequences change your shots regularly. Use a number of different shot sizes and angles to keep your sequences interesting. Although shooting a person at eye level is the most natural, this needn't be the only shot you use. Try different angles, vary the height of your camera to demonstrate different view points and avoid having people look directly into the camera.

Composition

Picture composition is all about organising the material in your shots in such a way as to communicate your ideas as effectively as possible, while at the same time keeping the pictures interesting and well balanced.

Close-up

53

Although sometimes difficult to achieve, the main rule regarding pictorial balance is known as the thirds rule. This rule divides your picture into a three-sections grid, both horizontally and vertically. When this has been achieved line up your shots so that the main features come at the intersections of your imaginary dividing lines. In this way the horizon in your scene should never fall on the centre line of the frame. It is also worth remembering never to shoot horizons which are not horizontal and to keep your verticals straight when tilting. Have a good look through your viewfinder to make sure there are no unwanted elements in shot. Remember to leave some 'looking space' or 'walking room' in front of your subject to reinforce the sense of direction on the screen, and always try to rehearse your shots.

To help pictorial balance and composition try using the thirds rule.

Because pictures are two-dimensional, it is very easy to confuse the eye with a bad choice of backgrounds. Nothing looks less professional then flowers or tele-

graph poles appearing from the top of a person's head (unless on purpose for comic effect) or strong horizontal lines appearing out of either ear. These may all seem very obvious errors but it is surprising how many people make them. There are several ways to obtain visual depth in your pictures. A diagonal composition leads the eye naturally to the centre of activity in the picture which a square-on shot fails to do. Movement is yet another method. People moving towards or away from your camera will create a sense of space and depth. When framing a scenic view using the branches of a tree in the foreground will also add depth to your shot.

Remember to leave some walking or looking room in front of your subject to reinforce the sense of direction.

Yes

55

At A Glance

1   The five main shots are the wide shot (WS), the long shot (LS), the medium shot (MS), the medium close-up (MCU), the close-up (CU).

2   Learn all about these shots and any additional shots as quickly as possible. Find out how they work and what they can achieve and convey to your audience.

3   Organise your material into interesting compositions.

4   Learn the 'thirds rule' and how to arrange your pictures on the screen.

5   Check your shots through the viewfinder to make sure you don't have trees growing out of the top of people's heads, or worse.

6   Don't forget to give your subjects walking and talking space.

7   Don't allow yourself to be fixed to any set of rules. Use them only as guidelines. Practise and experiment as much as possible – your film will be much better for it.

6

Panning, Tilting, Tracking and Zooming

A sure sign of a beginner's movie is that the shot is constantly on the move, swaying from side to side as if the camera had been given to a baby while his mother pushed him along in his pram. Unless you are being very clever you will use very few camera movements. Pans, tilts, zooms and, if you have the courage, tracking shots should cover it.

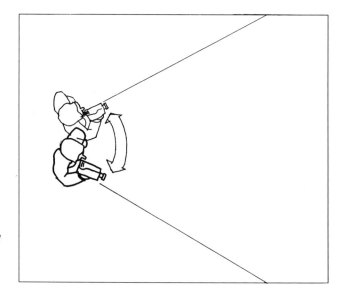

When panning your movement should be twice as slow as seems natural. It will feel odd at the time but will look good later.

Panning

Panning your camera involves swivelling it from left to right or right to left in a smooth gentle arc. The movement should be at least twice as slow as seems natural. It may seem odd at the time but will look fine when you review it later. It also allows your viewer time to take the scene in. The most effective pan covers an arc of no more than 90 degrees.

Your camera should remain static for a few moments at the beginning of your pan, and similarly, it should come to rest at the end of the shot, preferably on a point of interest and again remain there for a few moments. I would recommend about a 5-second pause at the beginning and end of each shot. That way if the pan goes wrong you can always use the start and end shots as single or additional shots later.

The pan is best used to scan subjects that are too large to get into a single shot, such as landscapes, a skyline or a large building such as the National Gallery. It can also be used to follow a walking figure or a speeding car, or to demonstrate the relationship between two things, for example panning from a screaming girl's face to the object of her terror or delight – a pop star, maybe. Always keep your subject sharply in focus. If you are filming a speeding car it doesn't matter if the background is blurred, in fact in some ways it is desirable as it helps give the effect of speed. What is important is that the vehicle is kept in focus. It is also important to keep your subject at the same point in the frame. The best position is not quite central but with more space in front of your subject than behind, giving him walking space.

Tilting

*Don't move your
pan too quickly or
you will blur your
shot.*

Tilting, as the word suggests, is just like panning but in
a vertical rather than a horizontal plane. The technique
is used to tilt from the bottom of a tall building, mountain or monument to emphasise its height or when
tilting down into a valley to reveal its depth. It may also
be necessary to use both a pan and a tilt to demonstrate
a particular scene which includes high mountains and
a wide landscape. It is also useful when following a
subject descending or ascending a building or wall.

The same general rules that apply to panning also
apply to tilting. Rehearse your tilt before shooting
to determine what your opening and closing shots will
be. When you have decided hold the beginning and
end images for approximately 5 seconds. Tilt slowly
and smoothly and in one direction (as with panning
nothing looks worse than the shot continually going
up and down or from side to side). When tilting up a
building where there is an exposure difference between
the start shot, which may be dark, and the end shot

61

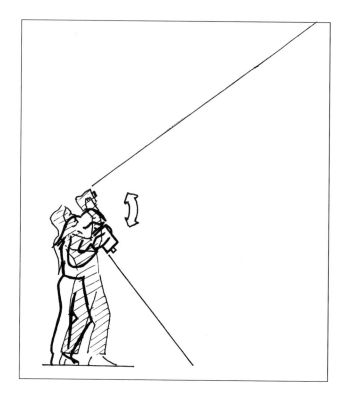

which will include the sky, check your exposer. There should be no problems if you have auto-exposer on your camera as the iris will compensate during the tilt. However if you have a manual control fix it to the first or front position and allow the sky to burn out.

Tilting can also make your shots far more interesting. For example, when you have a subject walking towards you and then pausing in medium close-up, it's quite common to set the camcorder at eye level, so that a pleasing composition is achieved at the end of the shot. However by setting the camcorder at a lower level and then tilting up as the character approaches, you can have a pleasing and constantly changing composition throughout the shot.

62

Tilt slowly and smoothly in one direction – nothing looks worse than shots continually going up and down or from side to side.

Tracking

This is the technique by which the camera is moved bodily backwards and forwards or alongside the subject. For this shot you will require some form of dolly. The professionals will lay tracks and have their camera mounted on a solid platform. However this is far too expensive a process for most of us. Try using a push-chair or pram. I have also found supermarket trolleys to be of great help. Tracking shots can also be taken from cars but results often depend on the state of the road surface. It is also a good idea to set the zoom to the widest possible angle: this will give the impression of speed even when the car is travelling slowly.

Zooming

For tracking shots try to use a dolly. If you don't have one improvise – it can be great fun.

Zooming is achieved by the movement of the lens to vary its focal length. You can control this movement manually or by using a built-in drive, which most

cameras have fitted as standard. While you are able to vary the speed of your zoom on some of the more sophisticated cameras, most cameras come with a fixed-speed zoom. Although fixed-speed zooms can limit creativity, they still produce good, smooth results. Take time learning how to use your zoom lens and get used to the different focal lengths it has to offer. You will find the slow zooms are the most demanding. If your operation is not smooth you will end up with a series of jerky movements.

You can use zoom shots to open and close your film. Start with a close-up of an object on a table and zoom back to reveal your presenter, or zoom past your presenter to the scenery or action beyond (again try to hold your start and end shots for about 5 seconds). You can also disguise the mechanical effect of the zoom by including other camera movements at the same time. A sweeping pan combined with a zoom out creates a smooth attractive finish.

When using your zoom as part of your film don't overdo it. Think about your shot and what you are trying to say in it to establish a relationship, to emphasise or dramatise a particular action. Zoom in on a child's face at the moment he opens his Christmas presents to capture a particular moment of pleasure. Zoom out from a ball being placed on a white spot to reveal the fact that a penalty kick is about to be taken during a football match. Avoid the dreaded 'Yo-Yo' shot, that is, the shot where the camera zooms in then zooms out rapidly. These shots always look awful, and can be irritating and confusing to your viewers. Use the zoom creatively to establish effects. If you zoom in quickly on your subject you will create a shock effect. On the other hand if your aim is to concentrate interest then zoom in slowly.

As with all things the more you practise and rehearse the better your results will be.

At A Glance

1   When panning, tilting or zooming keep your shots smooth and even.

2   Panning is best used to take in a scene like a landscape that can't be taken in a single static shot.

3   With both panning and tilting remember to hold your start and end shots for at least 5 seconds each.

4   Where specialist equipment is not available, improvise. Use supermarket trolleys, wheel chairs, etc.

5   Take your time and learn to use all the techniques properly.

6   Don't be frightened to experiment.

PART 2

Making your Programme

7

Ideas

Any idea can be a good one. The essence of the video camera is that it allows you to develop that idea and present it to an audience in an interesting and compelling manner. You are able to express your particular opinions on a subject, and, hopefully, draw your audience towards that view point. What I hope to do in the next few chapters is to introduce you to a few of the basics of programme making. Hopefully this will help you avoid many of the basic mistakes (which I often made) when making your own documentary or film.

Over the years film, and now video, has allowed people to strike back at a system which they feel has denied or frustrated them. It has allowed awkward and embarrassing questions to be asked of the authorities, and the means to broadcast their often inadequate replies to millions of viewers. For years the power to do this has been restricted to the few. Now with the advent of the cheap video camera and good quality video tape, the ability to make programmes has been made available to a much wider range of potential film makers. Although these programmes might not be able to reach the mass audiences of the major television companies, it does not make them any less significant. Its great potential as a grass roots political or social tool has been quickly realised. Armed with a video camera and a strong belief people are able to highlight issues which

Video cameras allow ordinary people a chance at self-expression normally denied them.

crucially affect their lives or community; video offers a method of self expression normally denied to them.

Team Effort

When done collectively making a video programme can create a strong feeling of community spirit. Anyone can enjoy it, from children in schools and clubs to elderly people in homes. Each person's input is important, and everybody can have a role within the crew. One person looks after the sound recording, another the camera or lighting. Others become directors or presenters, with each role interacting with another to help create a more professional-looking programme. With each successive production the responsibilities of each member of the crew can be altered, thereby giving each person a chance to test their skills at the various specialities, and allowing them to discover which they enjoy most.

70

Subject Matter

When developing your idea it is worth considering the following; do you have strong feelings about a certain subject? If so, who do you want to express those feelings to? Will your personal feelings unbalance your sense of fairness? Personal crusades usually don't make good programmes. Is there a subject that you are personally interested in and could that subject be of interest to others? If constructed properly any subject from stamp collecting to train spotting can entertain an audience. People often enjoy other people's interests, as programmes like *Video Diaries* have so often proved. Ideas are strange things; sometimes you have dozens and other times you have none. To help overcome this it's a good idea to keep an ideas notebook. As soon as an idea comes to you for a programme or ways to help you make that programme write it down. It will save you hours of 'now where did I see that?' later.

Armed with a video camera and a strong belief people are able to highlight issues which crucially affect their lives and community.

71

Try to keep a notebook with you at all times or you may forget all those ideas you had.

Remember your main objective in making any programme is to communicate your ideas to an audience in a fresh and convincing manner. I was always taught that the idea must always be the master, the technique the servant. The two questions to keep uppermost in your mind are:

1 does my idea entertain?

2 does my idea inform?

If the answer to both these questions is 'yes', you are essentially on the right track. If the answer is 'no', to either or both these questions, then it may be worth re-evaluating your idea. For example, what is the point of being informative, if your programme is so boring that people will either ignore it, or not appreciate the message you are trying to convey – the Yellow Pages is informative! Remember, no matter how unfair, your audience will probably compare your film with professionally made television programmes. Therefore the programme must be well thought through and constructed. Keep it short and to the point, make sure your idea is lively and imaginative, and that the direction is logical and properly argued. By following these basic rules, you are far more likely to communicate your ideas to an audience than with a programme that has been filmed in an unconstructed or haphazard manner.

You can have a good idea at any time and in any place – I often have mine in the bath.

73

Target your programme at a particular audience and establish early on the programme's objective. Decide in advance how you are going to develop your idea. Try to produce a written outline, thinking visually all the time. Research your subject thoroughly, becoming an expert on it. Your research should include people and locations, as well as the general concepts surrounding your idea. A poorly researched idea is as likely to ruin your programme as a badly directed one. Write your script and visualise it by producing a storyboard. Remember you are now working with a visual art and, as the cliché goes, 'a picture is worth a thousand words.' Link the script to the pictures as you move from sequence to sequence to see if the combination works. Finally, if you are working with a group develop your ideas and share them together. Everybody's ideas are worth considering and more often than not they will add a new and interesting dimension to the film.

At A Glance

1   Make sure your film both entertains and informs.

2   Keep it fresh and interesting.

3   Think visually all the time. You are not writing an essay.

4   Keep an ideas notebook.

5   Make films about subjects you either have strong opinions about or an interest in.

6   Target your programme at a particular audience and establish early on the programme's objective.

8

Research and the Recce

Before you start filming everything and everybody in sight, your programme idea will first need to be properly researched. Research is important for a number of reasons; it enables you to examine whether your ideas stand up or not; to see if there is enough material available to make a film; to establish which are the best people to talk to about your idea, and more importantly whether those people will talk to you. You will also need careful research to work out your filming schedules and budget.

When researching, become as expert in your topic as time allows. Given that normally the time you will have to make your film will be limited, you will only be able to include a few facts in your programme. Be ruthless, and choose only the most important and interesting facts to present in your programme. A film jammed with facts will leave your audience both bored and confused and they will quite simply stop enjoying it, or just turn off. It is also vital when researching your programme to think in pictures, or in sequences of pictures. Be continually on the look out for a shot or sequence of shots that will sum up the situation, and make a note of them in a notebook. Take a series of photographs of your locations and any interesting places that you think would help in the construction of your sequences.

When researching anything remember you are working with a visual art, so think in pictures.

The hardest thing about research is the amount of books and paperwork you have to wade through to get the information you need. There are hundreds of places you can search for information. Libraries, local government information offices, book shops, in fact any source that you can find that will be helpful in putting substance to your argument (again make a note of any sources you find that might come in handy on some other project later).

Discover which people will be able to talk about your ideas in an interesting manner before rushing around to see them with your crew, only to find out they are either not willing to take part in your programme, or if they are, cannot get the information across easily or coherently. Firstly try talking to your subject on the phone, or make an appointment to see him on your own. Take your time when interviewing your possible participant. He may well come up with an angle you had not considered, and even if he is not suitable for your

76

programme, he may put you in touch with people that might be. Although it is important to get as much information out of him as possible, always be polite, and as helpful to him as he is to you. Many interviewees will be either nervous or suspicious, so reassure them and try and form a relationship, it will make your job much easier.

After talking to all the people you feel are necessary, establish which people you feel made the best points and will be the most interesting to interview. Always try to see potential interviewees: there is a famous saying in television, 'they sounded okay on the phone.' If a boring person makes some interesting points you don't have to use them, you can always cover their points elsewhere in your script.

Take your notebook (or portable tape recorder) everywhere with you; you will find it invaluable when it comes to your interviews. Keep careful notes about your interview, to enable you to reflect on it later and

Try to see the person you want to interview. There is an old saying in television – 'He sounded all right on the phone.'

make decisions on who to include. Take as many details about your subject as possible, such as, full name (correct spelling), position held. Discuss the programme with him or her. See if she would mind taking part, and if she doesn't establish a time and location to do the interview. Consider anything that might make the day you have fixed awkward: school holidays, high tides, local football team are at home. Make a note of how to get to the location: you might know but the rest of the crew won't. Make a note of any equipment you will require, type of lights, lenses, etc. Given the weather in this country it's not a bad idea to have a back-up location that is under cover. A lot of effort and organisation can go into an interview, and it can be very irritating to have it interrupted by the rain.

Find out if there are any problems with the location, such as unwanted noises like low-flying aircraft, traffic, crowds of people. Even seemingly quiet locations can have problems. Microwaves, fridges, electric fans – all of these can emit sounds that can produce annoying hums on your sound track. See if they can be turned off

Before you turn up at your location make sure all permissions have been granted or you could find yourself in trouble.

78

or if there is some method of keeping them quiet. If you are filming outside you will need plenty of light, so find out what time it starts to get dark and plan your shoot accordingly. There is nothing more embarrassing, time consuming, or expensive than travelling out to a location only to find that half way through your filming you have to stop because you have lost the light. Check to see in what direction the sun will be. Note the position of doors and windows and the amount of natural light the room will receive during different times of the day.

You may also need permission to use certain locations; check this thoroughly, and if permission is required, find out who can give you that permission, and if possible try to get it in writing. Organisations like the police and local government officials can normally be very helpful. If you can get permission in writing, fine. If not make a note of who gave you permission and the time and date that permission was given. Failing everything find another location.

Preparing a briefing sheet for the crew outlining the time and place of interviews and shoots is essential. You will need to let them know where to park; where the toilets and refreshments are located; the location of the nearest bus stop, tube or train station. A small map of the location is also very helpful or, if the location is particularly difficult to find, arrange to meet at a certain point and drive to the location in convoy. Make sure you have spare batteries for your camera and that there is electricity for your lights. If you decide to use a presenter discuss likely questions with them and outline what you want out of each interview.

Work out the list of shots you want for each sequence and be as imaginative as possible. Try interesting positions and unusual angles, and always be on the look out for that one shot that sums everything up; a mother's love for her child, the different looks of the guests at a wedding. Try to film things that are happening or changing, and avoid having too many static shots in your film.

The Briefing Sheet

There are no hard and fast rules about briefing sheets. So long as all the information is there in a clear and understandable form it should do, though a map is sometimes a good idea. The most important thing is to get everybody you need at the right location at the right time, so make sure everyone who needs a copy gets one. Here is an example of a briefing sheet:

BRIEFING SHEET

All The King's Men

Time and Date	Location	Contact	Crew
2pm Friday 23 September 1991	York Cottage, Sandringham House.	Mr Francis 0603 5436	Camera: John Shoot Sound: Mike Yell Lights: B. Spark Director: Steve Point

Information:

Three interviews, two outside weather permitting and one inside.

Outside
1. Mr Nigel Stockton (35 yrs) who will be interviewed about the history of Sandringham.
2. Mr Hal Giblin (48 yrs) who will be interviewed about the Sandringham Company.

Inside
3. Mr Ashley Johnson (70 yrs) who will be interviewed about his father, who was killed with the Sandringham Company in August 1915.

Several power points for lights for inside interview. Interview to be conducted in sitting room of house which has only one small side window. If it rains then outside interviews to be moved to summerhouse inside the grounds. No power points but sufficient light. Lunch at the Dog and Duck pub at West Newton. Toilets: York Cottage.

No fees to pay.

All permissions cleared.

No additional insurance.

Directions to Location:

Take the A421 out of Norwich all the way to King's Lynn. At the main roundabout take the B721 to Sandringham. Follow signs to the royal estate. Approximately 100 yards past the main gate is a turning to your left which is sign-posted York Cottage. Follow the signs to the house. There is parking for up to 12 cars outside the cottage. If there are any problems call base on 0603 43267 or Mr Francis on 0603 5436.

The research and recce are as important to the programme as the direction or editing. If it is not done properly and with some imagination the programme will fail before it starts.

At A Glance

1 Every programme or film requires both research and a recce. Get to know as much about your subject as possible so you can decide which facts are and which are not vital to your film.

2 Always think in pictures and sequences.

3 Keep a book noting everything you do and the contacts you make. They may come in handy on another project.

4 Always talk to your possible interviewees before filming them to see if they are worth filming.

5 Check out your locations thoroughly. Have permissions been obtained? Are the locations noisy and what can be done about it? What types of power supplies are there? Are there any other possible problems, such as high tides, unwanted noises, etc.? Where are you going to park the crew's car and is there anywhere close by for refreshments? And what about the toilets?

6 Take photographs of the location and prepare a briefing sheet so that everybody can share in your hard work.

7 Consider your sequences and be on the look out for interesting shots.

8 Make sure everybody knows where and when to turn up.

9 Check, check and check again. The information you give your producer and director is the information they will use in the film. If it's wrong then they will look stupid and unprofessional and it will be your fault.

10 Make sure nobody expects to be paid for their services, that all permissions for filming have been obtained and you haven't breached any copyright.

9

Treatment and Storyboarding

The Treatment

Once the research and recce is finished the next stage is to work out a method of actually making your programme. The method normally used is to prepare a treatment.

To start with make a note of everything you want in your programme; putting things down on paper always helps concentrate the mind. Does your idea work? Have you done enough research and has it uncovered the information you wanted? How long will your programme last? Do you have enough sequences to fill that time and tell your story? In what order should those sequences be put together? Have you forgotten anything? How costly will it be? Does it inform and entertain? The treatment will also allow you to take stock from time to time, and examine in which direction your programme is going. Is it strong enough, is the programme getting your message across, and why are you making the programme in the first place? Having a good workable treatment will help make your programme a success.

The best method of doing this is to put the visuals on the left of the page and an indication of sound (commentary) on the right, as shown in this example:

The Big Match

Picture	Sound
1 Father and son getting ready for the match.	Commentary: It's a big day for John. His dad is taking him to his first football match.
2 John and his father walking to the football ground.	They live a long way from the ground and have to go by car.
3 Shot of John's father clipping up his seat belt.	John reminds his father to clip-up his belt.
4 Car driving towards ground.	John and his father can hear the crowds cheering long before they reach the ground.
5 Interview with John or voice-over.	I've never been to a football match before and am very excited, etc.
6 Shots of John and father going into ground through turnstiles.	John's father pays at the turnstile. John is only half-price.
7 Shots of football team and referee inspecting the ground.	There had been a hard frost the night before and the ground had to be checked to see if it was fit to be played on.
8 John and his father take their seats.	John is lucky. Because of new ground regulations the ground is now all seated.
9 Interview or voice-over by John. Cut-aways: general shots of the ground, the crowd, police, hot dog salesmen.	Most amazing place he had ever seen, etc.
10 Shots of the teams coming out onto the pitch. Roar of the crowd. Reaction of the crowd. John's reaction.	Finally the teams appear. John supports Nottingham Forest, the team in red. He's so excited at seeing his team for the first time he jumps up with excitement.

11 The kick off.	John now has to await the outcome of the game.
12 Music sequence in combination with shots of the play, crowd scenes and reactions. Follow the police, programme salesmen.	Music sequence; no commentary.
13 Half time. Drinking hot tea and eating sandwiches.	End of the first half. John's mum has packed them up well with hot tea and plenty to eat.
14 Interview with John.	What does he think of it so far? Who is his favourite player? etc.
15 Second half. More shots of the game, crowd, players, John and his father. Shots of any goals.	John's team scores first and takes the lead.
16 Shots of John's reaction at the end of the match.	The match is over and John's team has won – he is delighted.
17 End of the match. Pushing through the crowd.	The game is over and John makes his way home happy.
18 Arrives home. Interview.	Well, what did you think of it? etc.
19 End shot: people sweeping, cleaning football boots.	For John the match is over. For others next week's match is just beginning.

With experience you will soon be able to spot the strong and weak points in your story line. Just because you have done a treatment it doesn't mean that you have to stick to it rigidly. As your programme progresses you will have other ideas for shots and sequences. Some sequences you planned just won't work, others will be impossible to shoot. The treatment is just meant as a general outline which will hopefully make your programme much more interesting and professional.

To estimate the length of your programme try to judge the length of each sequence. Then add these sequences to arrive at your total. By allowing approximately 15 seconds for each point plus a proportion for any pictures without commentary it should give you the length of your programme. You can then make sure that all the points you want to make have been made and that you have made the best use of your available time. It's always best at this point to put more into your film than you may need: it's much easier to cut things out of a programme than to put them in at a later stage. You will also be able to estimate both the time you will have to film at each location and the number of shooting days it will take (don't forget to allow for travelling time). Make a list of possible questions before you start your interview (especially if you are not used to interviewing) to use as a guide, but don't feel you have to stick to them. You may think of a good question as you are interviewing, so be flexible (see chapter 11).

Storyboard

Storyboards are a vital part of the creative development of an idea. Designing a storyboard will furnish you with an overall plan from which you can order your shots later, often provide you with new ideas, and give you control over the shots and sequences you require. If you are inexperienced, there is no better way to develop your visual sense than by trying to storyboard every project you undertake. Translating what you have in mind into a series of images will help you to understand the visual potential of any project. It will also force you to think about what you are filming and why. Once you have outlined your general story, work out the details by drawing a storyboard, visualising each shot on

A Simple Storyboard

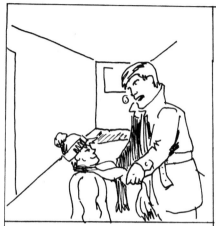

'It's a big day for John. His dad is taking him to his first football match.'

'They live a long way from the ground and have to go by car.'

'John reminds his dad to clip up his safety belt.'

'John and his father can hear the crowds cheering long before they reach the ground.'

'John's father pays at the turnstiles. John is only half-price.'

'John is lucky – because of new ground regulations the ground is now all seated.'

'John's team scores first and takes the lead.'

'The match is over and John's team has won. He is delighted.'

paper. Although this sounds complicated it's not, and you don't have to be an artist to make it work. Keep it simple; crude drawings can be as effective as artistic ones. All that matters is that you understand them. Number each picture, describing briefly below each illustration the type of action you have planned. You could also consider writing a small amount of commentary under each picture to help you match the two together ready for shooting. This can help you to remember what sequences you wanted and how long each one has to be.

Make sure that you have a strong story line and stick to the points you want to make. Whether it's the fire brigade trying out new life-saving equipment or the experience of a young boy going to his first football match, if your outline starts to become vague then your film will collapse and become dreadfully dull. Your audience will begin to ask (quite rightly), what's the point to all this? So keep to the point, keep it interesting and be clear about what you want to say.

At A Glance

1 When you have finished your research and are happy with it, prepare a treatment.

2 Put the proposed pictures on the left of your paper and the sound on the right.

3 Check your treatment. Read it over and over and think about it. Have you left anything out, does your idea work, and is there enough material to fill the amount of time you want your programme to last?

4 Estimate the duration of each sequence to give you an overall time for your programme.

5 Always allow for more time than you think you will need.

6 Does the programme entertain and inform and would Mr and Mrs Average watch and enjoy it?

10

Directing, and how to do it

An Introduction

Directing is the central pillar of film-making. It is nearly always considered separate to the other great film making skills of writing and editing, but really these are just an extension of directing. It is a common misconception that a director can come onto a project just before shooting, stick around for a few days and then pop their head around the cutting-room door every so often to see what the editor has made of their material, but nothing could be further from the truth. As a good director, your job will start long before you get on location with a camera, and end long after the rest of the crew goes home. You will be both artist and accountant, treading a narrow path between what you really want and what you can afford to get, as well as agony aunt and diplomat, deftly juggling to prompt fragile performers and contributors into giving their best. No one will work harder than you and no one will bear more responsibility, but no one will get more credit if things go well.

Getting What You Want

The art of directing can be summed up quite neatly as the art of *getting what you want*. It can be either very hard, or very easy, depending upon how far what you want differs from what's really happening, but it always comes back to the same, very simple thought. But that very simple thought hides probably the most complex and crucial part of a director's job, because before you can *get* what you want you have to *know* what you want. You would be surprised at how many directors, even professionals, get on location, or worse, get *off* location, before they realise they do not really know what they want from a sequence. You only have to go occasionally to the cinema or watch TV for a few nights to see examples of pieces shot without proper fore-thought – they look okay, they have all the right shots in them, but somehow instead of adding together to give a powerful piece, the images and the story are pulling in different directions, the sum is *less* than the individual parts. A few minutes thought about what a sequence is going to say in your finished film can tell you more than any number of books about how you should direct it.

In this chapter we will look at a few types of sequence that crop up regularly in films of all kinds and see what it is that you might want to get from each of them, and how you can direct them to make sure you do. Mostly, they are sequences that fall into the category of 'drama', that is, anything that happens *because* you've put the camera there, rather than 'documentary' which happens *despite* the fact that you put the camera there. However, the basic rules are the same, whether you are filming a car chase for an action adventure, or a family wedding for posterity.

The Action Sequence

It is useful to deal with action sequences first because not only do they often occur, cut to music, as an opening of a film, but also because in directing them you will have to overcome many of the most fundamental problems of film making. To begin with, filming a convincing action sequence will be the hardest of all your tasks as a director, but the good news is that a few basic rules will transform awkward and unrealistic first attempts into slick, believable movie-style action. And remember, the mark of a well-directed sequence is that no one will notice any directing!

The basic rule of action filming is *cover the action*. That means, make sure you have filmed the sequence of action from enough angles so that you will be able to edit together shots that will tell the story, but will also allow you to condense the time-scale over which things are really happening. For instance, filming someone coming into a kitchen and making a cup of coffee would take forever if you decided to cover it only from one angle – you would then be stuck with having to wait for the kettle to boil. But if you have filmed it from two angles, and one of them is framed so that the kettle isn't visible, you will be able to concertina the time by cutting from one shot to the other perhaps giving the coffee-maker something to do, like getting the mugs from a cupboard, or searching for a teaspoon, in order to distract the viewer from the boiling kettle. This concertinaing of time is crucial to the film maker's art. It allows the director to show only the pieces of action that are relevant to the sequence, in a minimum of time.

Covering the action from a number of angles, however, can throw up some real headaches for the unwary director. For instance, a 'master shot' or establishing shot from one angle and a covering shot from a similar one are unlikely to cut together smoothly. Always change the camera position enough to make the shots significantly different if you want the cut from one position to the other to look smooth (or better still, not to be noticed at all). One trick is to change the size of the shot: if you have shot a master wide shot (WS) of the kitchen first, perhaps a head-and-shoulders shot or mid shot (MS) will work well for the covering shot. Try it to see what you like the look of. You will find that changing *both* the angle and the size may work best – a cut from a wide shot to a closer shot from the same camera position often looks odd.

Another problem you are likely to encounter as soon as you start shooting a scene from a number of angles and consequently, a number of times, is continuity. Most people, when they think of continuity, think of problems like 'which hand did the actor use to pick up the kettle?' and, certainly, continuity problems like that need watching. But a bigger, and often less noticeable problem on a shoot is continuity of action. Imagine the kitchen sequence. In the wide shot the coffee-maker plugs in the kettle and turns to the cupboard to pick out some mugs. You choose this as the moment you will cut to a shot from the other side of the room, this time tighter, a mid shot. When you have repositioned the camera, you tell the coffee-maker to pick-up the action from the moment you imagine the cut taking place, say just as they open the cupboard door. The coffee-maker dutifully waits, poised in position until you say 'action!' – it all goes swimmingly well, and then on to the next scene.

It is only when you get into an editing room that the problem will hit you: by stopping the action in one place in the wide shot, and picking it up at exactly the same point in the action in the mid shot, you have left yourself no flexibility whatsoever. You *have* to cut from wide to mid shot at exactly that point, regardless of whether it looks right or not. The action is also unlikely to look natural: any performer, even the finest, would be hard pushed to start a supposedly continuous piece of action, like taking mugs out of a cupboard, midway through and look convincing from the first frame. The secret is always to overlap the action – if the wide shot ends with opening the cupboard door, let the action continue a little further before saying 'cut!', and pick up the action in the mid-shot from a little earlier, *before* the coffee-maker gets to the cupboard door. That way you will have an overlap of several seconds and you can pick the smoothest point in the action to cut from one shot to the other – the action will look continuous, as if there were two cameras filming the same scene.

One final thing that all good directors and cameramen should be wary of when filming a sequence from many angles is a trap that is easy to fall into and can produce very confusing results. To explain it in the most obvious case, imagine filming a wedding. The bride and her father are walking down the aisle. You have put the camera on the right as you look towards the altar. Through the lens the couple appear to move from the left of frame across to the right. When they have left the frame you rush around the back to the left-hand side of the church. This time through the lens the couple enter on the right and walk across to the left. On their own, both shots will look fine, but cut together in the way you had intended, the bride and her father will appear to walk across the frame from one side to the other, disappear briefly from view and then walk back again in the opposite direction! Dramatically this may give quite the wrong impression.

What you have inadvertently done is to *cross the line*. The line in question is an imaginary one drawn along the ground in the direction the couple are walking, in this case, straight down the centre of the church. The rule is, always film them from the same side of the line, never cross it. What that means in practice is, unless you specifically want to give the impression someone or something has done a u-turn, always keep them moving in the same direction on screen. In the church example it's easy to see how confusing the result of crossing the line can be. The same would obviously be true in filming a chase sequence, for instance – one would not be sure who was chasing whom and where. But sometimes it is much less clear that one has broken the rule and one is struck simply by the fact that a cut between two shots looks odd. Often, simply being aware of the problem and thinking of the cut sequence in your head

93

Beware crossing the line, otherwise your film will look slightly ridiculous.

as you frame up your shots is enough to ensure you don't fall into any traps but, if you are really unsure, do what all good directors do when struck by doubt – film it both ways and decide later! Another tip to avoid potential problems in the cutting room is to film some shots where the subject turns around in the frame. So, if you are shooting a sequence with a car speeding along country roads, try to shoot a scene at a corner so that the car enters on one side of the frame, turns and leaves on the same side. This shot can easily be used between two shots that theoretically 'cross the line' but, linked by the turning shot, the visual effect will be fine.

Crossing the line is one of the most feared and least understood problems in directing, but really, once you are aware of it, there is nothing to worry about. As you get more advanced, you may even find that crossing the line gives some effects that work very well dramatically. You might also try to keep an eye on TV and cinema to see how professional directors tackle the problem.

Once you have mastered the basics of getting what you want, covering the action, overlapping it where appropriate and avoiding crossing the line, you will be able to concentrate on making sure you are getting the most out of the sequence. Remember your basic principle – *What do I want this sequence to say?* One question to ask yourself is 'How much of what is happening do we need to know?' For instance, if the action consists of someone getting into a car, is it important that we know where the car is? Do you need a wide shot to establish that it is in a leafy, suburban street, or alone on a windswept clifftop? Alternatively, if the scene is to be dramatic and intriguing – perhaps a car theft? – maybe you don't want *any* wide shot: shoot it all as a series of close-ups. You will find that the more you think about a scene, the more of the directing decisions are made for you: for instance, you may be filming someone getting into the driving seat of a car from the passenger's viewpoint. Clearly then, it is

95

vital that the master shot of the sequence is filmed with the camera inside the car looking at the driver approaching. Alternatively, if the sequence is about someone leaving whilst watched by a distraught mother or lover from inside a house, perhaps the master shot should be from their point of view? The more you do, the more different ways you will find of filming a sequence. You will also be surprised by how little you need to show in order to get over the point of what is happening – you won't, for instance, need to show the driver of the car get the keys out of their pocket, unlock the door, adjust the lumber support of the seat and fasten the seat-belt before they pull off, even though they may do this every time. You may find you don't even need to show them getting into the car at all.

One final thing to mention in shooting action: don't use the zoom. If you want to get a closer look, move closer or cut to a zoomed-in close up. Zooming is an odd effect visually. When working with a camera you are trying to show what your eyes might see, and your eyes do not zoom. I find that a zoom draws attention to itself: it says 'this is not real life, it is a film'. That is a real problem if you are seeking to make convincing drama. I find a zoom is only acceptable when filming documentary footage – i.e. real life. When what you are filming is obviously really happening, maybe a birth or a wedding or a school sports day, it doesn't matter that you remind the audience that they are seeing things through the eyes of a camera, but otherwise it is a mistake. It is like the actors in a play catching the eye of someone in the audience – the spell of realism is broken.

Shooting Documentary

Directing documentary is something of a contradiction in terms. When you are striving to capture what is really happening (as opposed to drama when you are filming what you have *made* happen) the best direction is often *not* to direct. This is a perfect example of the idea that a director's job is much more than just telling people what to do on set.

In documentary, the skill of a director is to set up a situation and to get access to situations and simply to film what happens, rather than to try to control what happens. This might seem to go against the principle of getting what you want, but in fact, it doesn't mean you don't get what you want, it just means that you need to go about getting it in a different way, or even that you need to reconsider what it is you do want and try wanting something else!

Let me illustrate this with an example. How can you exercise control on something that is not only inherently uncontrollable, but on something that the very act of controlling will destroy? Take, for instance, the ultimate uncontrollable thing, an animal. Suppose that the documentary I want to direct is about dogs driving taxis. I can try till I am blue in the face to make this film but I am unlikely to get very far. I could resort to training a dog to drive a taxi, but then I have not made a documentary but a drama – things are happening *because* of the camera, rather than *despite* the camera.

Much better would be to reconsider what documentary I should be making. Perhaps I would be better off making a film about dogs burying bones? Obviously this is an extreme example, but I believe that good documentary is observational: you direct the situation only in so much as you chose what you will to film, or what situation you will put your subjects in. Once you have got that far, you observe, and bite your tongue when you want to stop people and get them to do something again because you missed it. If you want to control their every move, you should be making a different film.

The Art of Being Bloody-minded

As you keep trying different things with your camera you will learn to shape films in a more and more sophisticated way. Whilst the rules in this chapter will help, never be bound by them: in film making the only value of knowing the rules is so that you can be aware you are not following them! However, never forget the basic principles: what do you want to get and why do you want it? And remember, whilst you may have a team around you as dedicated to the cause as you are, only you really know what it is that you want. *Make sure you get it!* It may be difficult at times to ask people to do the same scene over and over again when they have done it six times already and cannot see what was wrong, but if it wasn't what you wanted and you know what to do to make it better, do it. It may be difficult at the time, but it will be a whole lot harder later. If there is one truly unpleasant thing about being a director, it is sitting in a cutting-room looking at your film and saying 'If only . . .'

At a Glance

1   Think about the shots you want beforehand and make sure you get them.

2   Make sure you film your sequence from enough angles to make your edit easier and more interesting.

3   Beware of crossing the line, otherwise your film will look very bizarre.

4   Think carefully before you use your zoom: be sure there isn't a better alternative.

5   Keep the continuity flowing, giving your sequence a more natural flow.

11

Script and Commentary

When you have all those wonderful pictures to look at, who needs words? But words can give those pictures meaning and drive the programme forward, so it is important to get them right; finding the correct balance isn't easy.

The very first decision you have to make is whether you want any commentary (or 'voice over' as it is sometimes referred to) in your programme at all. You could just mix the sound effects, music and interviews you have taken, but that is particularly difficult, and although it is good at getting across impressions, is not suitable for conveying clear and concise information.

Having opted for words, whatever you do, control yourself! Words have a habit of multiplying once they see a page; you see a blank page and you feel you have to fill it. Resist! As a trainee film maker I was constantly demanding more time in my programme for the script, convinced that the world would be totally unable to understand the pictures in front of its eyes unless the commentary spelled it out for them. Pictures of course can speak for themselves, and a programme with acres of script is likely to be too heavy. Television is not radio with pictures put in to cover the blank screen – don't feel you have to cover your film with words.

Once you've got your urge to write under control, the next problem is what comes first – the pictures or the script? Well, it's a bit of both really. Making a programme is a blend of pictures and words and they have to show each other respect. That may sound obvious, but you would be amazed how many TV presenters seem to ignore the way pictures and words go together, just covering the words with anything as long as it doesn't look out of place. The fact is that usually the camera person or the video tape editor have great ideas about how your masterpiece is going to look, whilst whoever is writing the script will be head down at a typewriter focusing only on what the item is going to say. For goodness sake, talk to each other early on, so each of you has an idea of what the others want to achieve.

One way to get everyone on the same wavelength is to do a pre-shooting script. Script should develop and improve each step of the way when you are making a programme, but you need to start somewhere. Before you go out shooting, jot down a few facts for voice overs and put together an outline script. It doesn't even have to be full sentences, just an idea of what you want to say in this particular piece of the programme, how long you think this particular voice over will be, and what things you will be referring to specifically. It will help you focus your ideas as to what your programme is about and how you intend to script it. It also gives the camera person an idea of what shots to get, how long those shots should be to cover the voice over, and will give him or her a general feel for what you want to achieve. The edit is no place to find out that there are no pictures of an aircraft taking off if your final script suddenly decides the programme will be a total disaster unless you write a piece about planes zooming off the tarmac. It's no good being vague, hoping that you will be able to rescue your film in the edit by finding a picture which 'might just fit' if 'people don't look too closely'. There's a word for that sort of thing: 'wallpaper', laying down shots of anything you think you can get away with. Always remember that the pictures

100

and script are like body and soul, not second cousins twice removed. Make sure your camera person knows what you might be saying in your script, so the right pictures can be taken.

When all the shooting has been done, make sure you take time to watch the results before rushing into your final commentary. You may have a pre-shooting script you are happy with, and the camera person may have

Always try to provide information in your script that isn't obvious from the picture.

After years of searching Tim finally found the old hall. He knew his great-grandfather had worked there and died locally. Would his great-grandfather have been buried in the local churchyard, and would this be the end of his search?

He decided to search the Victorian graveyard. It was quite a task as many of the stones were damaged or worn out.

101

Then suddenly there it was: his search was at an end. He had found the final resting place of his ancestor.

Shot of headstone. Interview about how Tim feels at coming to the end of his search.

got every shot you feel you need to cover what you intend to say, but there can be inspiration in your pictures, and it would be foolish to ignore them. Something may have happened whilst the camera was running that you hadn't expected. The lighting in a shot you only planned to use a snatch of might have been so good that you might want to expand that section to lengthen the shot, or conversely, the picture could be so poor you can't use it to cover the commentary you had in mind, and so will have to cut that voice over down. It sounds like common sense, but some TV people don't write to pictures at all. They just bash out their scripts and deliver them to the editor, like Moses coming down from the mountain with their sacred text, and tell them to 'cover it'. Pictures and words must have respect for each other because they can inspire each other.

When commentating on a film don't feel you have to cover your entire programme with words. Let the action speak for itself.

103

Once you have viewed the pictures and made the necessary alterations to your pre-shooting script, hopefully you will feel full of ideas and phrases, all just desperate to get written down on paper. The danger is that you will end up writing something appropriate for an English language exam that will sound awful as commentary. The reason is that English-as-it-is-written is very different to English-as-it-is-spoken. The creative writing and the sentence structure that wins such glowing praise in English lessons, or even from a book or newspaper editor, just won't work here. Just think about what is going to happen to your script. Someone is going to read it aloud, and the viewer will hear someone talking to them. What you have got is one side of a conversation, so any programme script should not sound out of place if it were spoken by someone talking to someone else in a bus queue, for example.

It is hard to come to terms with this because the way we have been taught makes us use one set of language rules when we put our thoughts down on paper, and another when we open our mouths. Script writing is initially like asking your brain to use the wrong set of rules; it's hard to come to grips with it at first, but there is an easy way to get it right. All you have to do is read aloud what you have written, either to yourself or to someone else. Do you feel strange saying it? Does the other person think you sound strange when you say it to him? If so, you may pass your English language exam, but you'll fail the script-writing test because the viewer's attention will be attracted to how peculiar the words being spoken in the programme are, and so their attention will be drawn away from what the words are actually saying, and what the pictures are showing. It's worth spending a bit of time on this because it is important to get it right. Perhaps the worst offender is the subordinate clause. In a newspaper article for example, it is quite acceptable to write:

> *The crowd, already infuriated by the lack of com-*
> *mitment from the team, went wild when the visitors*
> *scored twice in the last five minutes.*

Now, we don't speak like that. If the voice over was going to say that the crowd was getting pretty livid, it would be more natural to say:

> *The crowd was already furious because the side just*
> *didn't seem to be trying, so when the visitors scored*
> *twice in the last five minutes, they went wild.*

Alliteration is another literary device that may win prizes for the written word, but sounds decidedly odd when uttered in conversation on the 8.10 from Hove to Victoria. That means it isn't right for the voice over either:

> *The wet, windy, winding way reduced our group to*
> *a miserable rabble within minutes of setting off.*

Poetic, isn't it? And it beautifully and effectively creates strong images of what the walkers were experiencing as they started out on their journey. But the point about television is that the viewers can actually see the conditions, so you don't need to waste precious seconds in your voice over telling them what is before their very eyes, especially if it is said in a way that sounds very unusual. Use the help the pictures give you to put in more information that isn't obvious from what the viewers are watching, but will help them understand the pictures more.

For example:

> *Within minutes we were drenched, and the fact that*
> *we still had ten miles to go meant we were doubly*
> *depressed.*

The walkers were obviously unhappy because, let's say, the pictures showed the wind almost knocking them over and the rain pouring down their faces, but

Try not to be too literal in your descriptions – 'Here we have the Lord Privy Seal.'

the script gives an extra reason for them being so miserable. They had another ten miles of this to put up with!

Of course there is room for creative writing when writing commentary, but it has to be handled very carefully indeed, and it comes in the relationship between pictures and word. Say you are making a piece about the fishing industry, and you want to talk about the Germans buying more fish from us. Your script might say:

> *Faced with falling fish sales at home, the British fishermen have found a new market in Germany.*

Quite acceptable, and you could cover it with pictures of people buying fish in German shops. But just a bit of creative thinking, and you can improve on it. For instance, it you have film of full nets coming out of the sea and pulleys straining to land the catch, there is a

106

good action shot that would be far more visually exciting for the viewer. You could use it just by wording your script a bit more carefully to accommodate this picture:

> *Despite poor sales at home, new markets are beginning to emerge in Germany for British fisherman.*

The nets coming out of the sea would come up when the voice over said 'emerge', so we have new markets emerging in the script and nets emerging from the sea. The picture has inspired the writer to do something different, and it becomes a metaphor for the point being made in the script.

Making the script sound interesting is obviously mainly down to the person who is going to voice it, but there are a lot of things the writer can do to help her. Once again, remember that what we are talking about is part of a conversation going on between the commentator and the viewer, so think about the way we talk to each other and the sort of phrases that we use which can make conversations more animated. One basic device is simply the word 'now' to start a sentence. It gives the impression of immediacy, and makes the viewer sit up and listen a bit more:

> *Now, here is a problem that is going to take years to solve.*

It is a chatty style that many people use in conversation to grab attention, so why not use it occasionally in script writing? Another phrase people sometimes use to make a point more firmly and to draw people's attention to a specific detail is:

> *What we've got here, is . . .*

Again, it is a friendly, chatty line which makes the voice over more natural. A third trick is to give a fanfare to something coming up. At its most extreme, someone might say 'You're going to love this' before launching into something they feel is of interest to everybody. You have to be a bit more subtle when you're making programmes:

What happened next took us all by surprise.

or,

Look what happened here when our cameras arrived.

How far you can go with this depends on what sort of programme you are making. Not all programmes can take a chatty style; perhaps you want something a little more formal. It is up to you to decide what the tone of your piece is, but remember, whatever you choose, it has to sound natural.

Finally, when do you use voice over to get the best out of it? Obviously it outlines the story you want to tell, but it also gets you out of trouble when you are editing. It can summarise a vital point made by someone you've interviewed, but whose answer is too long or too boring to use. It can improve the question the interviewer asked, by replacing it and making it shorter, more precise, and it can make sense of vague answers you feel you have to use. 'It is good/bad/inspiring/tragic' creates problems, because what is 'good/bad/inspiring/tragic'? What is this mystery 'it'? The question should provide the information, but perhaps you don't want to use the question in the finished programme for some reason. A short voice over link such as 'The new sports hall is so striking, everyone has an opinion about it', would get round the problem.

Introducing interviewees is another use for voice overs, but don't think you have to introduce everyone. Captions over the picture of the person can give basic information like 'David Wyatt, football coach', and you could go straight to his answer about his views on the sports hall after the 'everybody has an opinion about it' commentary. Occasionally though, you need more. Background information can help to give the person, and therefore their answer, more weight. You might say:

> *David Wyatt has been coaching school sides across Britain for 20 years, and believes this new sports hall is the best he's ever seen.*

Used carefully, voice over is a godsend; it can help you tighten up rambling answers, enable you to use only the best bits of interviews, and add new insights into the relevance of answers or the impact of pictures. Remember though, use it sparingly, make sure it is clear and in harmony with the pictures and you'll have a video script rather than just a piece of writing.

And Cue . . .

Once it is written to your satisfaction read it against your pictures, this time making a note on the script of your *in* (the time to start speaking to your pictures) and *out* points (the time to stop speaking). It is a great help when editing your programme to make sure that you have got a friend with you who can cue you in and out. Make sure you rehearse before you start to dub your voice over the pictures. Even at this late stage you will find you will still have to make corrections to your script to make it fit properly. Choose somewhere quiet to do your dub and when cueing use the word 'and' so that the commentator has plenty of time to prepare and comes in on time. 'And cue' you will find will be two of the most important words you will learn when it comes to the practicality of dubbing your script over the pictures.

At A Glance

1 Choose your words carefully, and make each one count.

2 Keep your sentences short, simple, and to the point.

3 When matching your script against the length of your pictures remember you speak at about three words per second.

4 Commentary should be used to explain awkward visual sequences, or when the pictures don't seem to make sense. For example, when cutting from the South American Jungle to a children's hospital ward, the pictures may seem bizarre. However if in commentary you explain that rare jungle plants are being used to develop medicines for sick children then it all makes sense.

5 Be constantly on the look out for good commentary points.

6 Don't describe. There is nothing worse than telling your audience what they can see for themselves.

7 When examining your pictures consider what words might add information to them. If there aren't any then don't force it.

12

Interviews

All your life you've been answering other people's questions: your parent's, the teacher's, an employer's. Now you have the chance to be the question master, but don't get carried away. There's more to asking questions than asking questions.

There are four areas I want you to think about when it comes to doing an interview: the preparation, the time immediately before the interview starts, the interview itself and finally the way the interview is directed. There are important points to remember at each stage, and they cover everything from actual questions asked to the way you ask them and the setting for the interview. The first thing you must realise is that a television or video interview is more than just words; the pictures have to be right as well.

As in most things, preparation is vital. Don't just think you can march in and wing it or you could end up looking foolish, or have nothing suitable for your programme, which is even worse. Right at the beginning think carefully about what sort of answers you want. This may sound like putting the cart before the horse, but this way it will give you a clear idea of what you are after so that you won't waste a lot of tape interviewing people you don't eventually use. Let's say you are making a programme about a school project. Think what you want in it. You might want to hear why people are doing the project in the first place, how it works, what it hopes to achieve, what the results are and whether it has a future or will be left to gather dust. Once you have got an idea of the points you want to make, look around for the people who are in the best positions to make them. This research is vital because there's nothing worse than recording an interview where the interviewee keeps saying, 'Sorry, I don't know', or just gives a few monosyllabic answers before being totally overcome by nerves and shutting up entirely. Don't be put off if you don't get the answer you wanted, or if the answer you do get is too obscure. Keep going. If necessary ask the same question in a different way until finally you get the reply you wanted. Again, preparation can save you hours.

Researching Your Questions

Once you have worked out who you want to interview and are satisfied as much as you can be that they will make good interviewees, make sure you research the subject you are going to ask questions about. Yes, I know you're not the person giving the answers, but I assure you there are several good reasons for knowing your subject. Firstly, how can you ask the key questions that get right to the heart of the issue or event if you don't know much about it in the first place? Research may well enable you to dig up little gems of information which will help give your piece a twist. For example, your programme is about a school project involving having to climb a cliff to collect something to analyse. If you found out in your research that one of the class suffered slightly from vertigo, an interview with the person about how to cope with that fear would add a new dimension to your piece. Don't depend on your interviewee too much to deliver the goods either. In the heat of the moment during the interview they may forget to say something crucial about the project, or even want to hide something about how the project went wrong, took weeks to mend and went disastrously over budget so that next term's science class won't be able to have any new microscopes! Thorough research will enable you to cope with that in the interview by reminding them of crucial points they have 'forgotten'.

Finally, think about it from the position of the person being interviewed. If through your very basic and unperceptive questions the interviewee sees you quite clearly know nothing and understand even less about what you are asking, what are they going to think? 'Why should I bother with you if you can't even be bothered to find out a bit about what I'm talking about?' They could walk out in disgust, sulk or be patronising in their answers. The fact that you took trouble instead to do research will flatter them, and they will feel more at ease talking to you, and this will show in the interview.

Armed with all this knowledge you can write out your questions. Start with a few easy, basic questions, ones that you perhaps don't even have any intention of using in the final edited programme. It's not a waste because it helps settle the person being interviewed and gives them confidence. You may have been chatting quite happily to that person seconds before the camera turns on and starts to record, but as soon as it does everything changes. Everyone goes quiet and the interviewee may well feel caught like a rabbit in a headlight, with you, the evil question master, about to grill him. It is a very unnatural situation, and a few questions such as, 'You must be very pleased with the interest in the project' or 'Did you always want to work in schools?' will help settle them. By the time you reach question four the interviewee should be in his stride, and you can start asking the questions you feel are vital for the programme.

All prepared, you turn up on the day, but there is still work to be done before the interview starts. Even though your mind is probably on the questions, think pictures for a moment. Where should the interview take place? A background that has something to do with what you are talking about is usually a good idea. The trouble is that often all you have time for is to interview someone seated at a desk. It is also the most simple option in that the room will probably be quiet and the person being interviewed won't mind you moving the furniture around to get the best angle. If you can though, look for alternatives: risk being creative!

If your project is a scientific one, the obvious place would be to do the interview in a science lab with the equipment in full view. If animal welfare is the subject of the programme, then how about doing the interview in front of a field of cattle? Beware of the dangers associated with arranging outside broadcasts, when you bravely go forth mike in hand to venture where more experienced commentators would avoid. Planes and lorries will appear as if by magic, gangs of small children all determined to make their mark and appear on television to impress their parents will pull faces behind

Try to keep your background relevant to the subject you are talking about, i.e. if the interview is about parkland have parkland as the setting.

your interviewee. Even adults will try to stand in shot shouting 'Hello Mum' or worse. Be brave. If the interview is short, or if the interruptions are relevant, then go for it. An interview about the problem of living next to a main road will be helped by having to raise your voice a bit to talk above the rumble of the traffic, whilst an interview about new play equipment for a school will benefit from the sight and sounds of the playground behind the shot. But always make sure that the viewer gets to see where all the noise is coming from so they can put sight and sound together.

Once you have chosen the location spend the last few moments whilst the camera, sound and lights are being set up to go over your questions. See if there's anything you've missed or try to memorise the questions so you don't spend the interview with your head buried in your notebook looking to see what comes next. Have a friendly word with the interviewee. They may well be worried about the way they look, what they will say, and especially what you are going to ask them. Almost always they will want to know the questions before the interview starts. Don't tell them. They will only start to worry about a particular question, try to work out answers in their mind and try to remember what they had thought of when it comes to the real thing. Their answers will invariably be confused and won't be spontaneous. By all means give them a brief outline of the question areas, such as 'Well, we'll start off chatting about what the project is about and take it from there.' But be as vague as possible.

Filming an Interview, the TV News Way

The object is to make the interview look like it was filmed with more than one camera (invariably, unless in a studio, they are not). The first (and most important)

115

thing to film is the interviewee's answers: these are, after all, the reason why you are filming anything at all. The common technique is to sit him or her in a chair (not a swivel chair as people have a distressing habit of rocking side to side as they get nervous) and to place the camera about six feet away. The interviewer (often the director) should sit with his head as close to the camera as he can comfortably get. This means that the interviewee can look directly at the interviewer (so they feel comfortable in that they are talking to a person and not a lens) and yet their 'eyeline' (where they are looking) is close enough to the camera that the effect on scene is still pleasing. In general it is a bad idea to get people to speak directly to the camera (like a TV presenter would), though many people often think this is what they should do. Often it is next to impossible to stop your interviewee giving the camera sidelong looks, or turning to it to finish their sentences, but you should do everything you can to stop them because the effect on screen is very unnerving. (In practice, the best way to stop people doing this is to look directly into their eyes, nod a lot and make a big show of being interested in what they are saying. Don't, however, be tempted to say 'mmm . . .' and 'Yes, I know' as this will make editing the answers together nearly impossible.)

A good habit to get into when filming interviews is to change the size of the shot of your interviewee from wide shot to mid shot to close-up. This is useful for two reasons: first because it is more dramatic to be on a close-up if the interview gets intense or emotional, whereas a wide shot is best for summaries or general information and secondly because, just as in action sequences, you will be able to cut from one shot to the other and, because of the size change, the cuts should look relatively smooth. In order to get the shot size changes do not bother moving the camera to a different position, just change the shot size with the zoom. The best time to do it is whilst the interviewer is asking a question as the chances are you will not want to include

116

*Medium close-up –
the master interview
shot.*

his questions in the cut film, only the interviewee's answers. (It is often worth mentioning this fact to your interviewee. Ask her to repeat your question in the first line of her answer and avoid asking questions that need to be answered with a yes or no.)

Many director/camera-operator teams have a visual code worked out between them and the director will signal whether he or she wants to make the shot tighter, perhaps if the question is probing a deep or emotional point, or whether the camera-operator should loosen off.

Asking and Listening

Now we come to the interview itself, and I want to divide this up into the technique of asking the questions, and the technique of listening to the answers.

117

Let's take the listening bit first because you may feel the last thing you want to be taught about in a chapter about asking questions is how to listen. Think a moment about what is happening. The person being interviewed may be seen by numerous people, but for the interview itself, the only audience he notices is you. When we talk to each other normally we pick up signs from the listener about how we are doing. It is exactly the same in a recorded interview. If you spend your time looking at your questions or at your feet, the interviewee will start to feel uncomfortable, feel that perhaps what he is saying is boring. The person needs visual come back signs from you to encourage him, he needs a person to talk to, not a brick wall. Look at him as if you are interested, but don't get into a staring match with him.

Don't just pretend to listen either. He may say something you hadn't expected which raises new points you have to ask about. His answer may be too long, too short or just very dull, and you need to be listening to make sure it is right. He might absentmindedly use a wrong name or say something he doesn't really mean. I promise you, even people used to being interviewed can get words muddled and say they like a thing, when in fact what they meant to say was they didn't like it. It is no good spotting the mistake days later when you are viewing your rushes (tapes). You have to be listening, editing in your head during the interview. Remember the person may be very important to your film so if you get it wrong you may have to do the interview again which can take up a lot of time you may not have and can add to the total cost of the programme. Even worse you may not get a second chance at the interview.

Finally there is the technique of asking the questions. Remember you are the one in control. Your subject may be the Prime Minister but you are asking the questions, you decide when the camera starts and stops, you are the boss. Be confident in the way you ask questions,

118

but not arrogant; you don't want the interviewee to see you as an opponent or else she will become defensive, even be aggressive and then he won't feel relaxed, which is what you want.

Being in control you have the power to stop the interview whenever you want. This is extremely useful, and can get you out of tricky situations. Most people assume you start an interview and keep recording, asking the questions, listening to the answers, until you have asked all you want to ask, but you have more flexibility than that. If the interview isn't going well, tell the interviewee that you want to stop recording for a moment whilst you fix an imaginary camera or lighting fault. Then go over where they are going wrong; the answers may be too long or they may be getting too nervous and need reassurance and a friendly chat before continuing. You can of course break in whilst the camera is recording and ask them to do their answer again if it isn't quite what you want. Don't do it too often because it becomes unnerving, but if you get a vital question, one you know you want to use the answer to, then you must have another go. Say gently, 'Yes, that's fine, but I wonder if we could do it again because the point you are making is a very good one, but it needs to be a little shorter/clearer/more detailed for the piece.' That way you won't offend the interviewee, who usually trusts the interviewer about what will and won't work.

One final point before I get to the questions themselves. Usually you want the answers 'clean'. By that I mean your questions shouldn't be starting or trailing off over your interviewee's answers. It makes it a nightmare to edit if you want to join one answer to another, or if you want to do a programme where the interviewer's voice isn't heard at all. Of course, you could do a programme where interruptions by the person asking the questions are exactly what you want! This style creates energy, is exciting and challenging, but be clear in your mind what sort of question style fits your programme before you start the interview. If you want clean answers, and if the question and answer overlap, don't be afraid to jump in, and ask the question again.

What to Ask and How to Ask It

Take out of an interview only what you need and disregard the waffle. You can cover the joins with cut aways. In this example you need use only the speech in italics.

Transcript of interview with Councillor John Herbert, Environmental Officer, Nottinghamshire County Council.
23 December 1992. Interview outside Gamstone Farm, Gamstone Lane, West Bridgford, Nottingham.

Q. Despite three public enquiries going against the council why are you persisting in trying to build an industrial park on this Green Field site?

R. First of all I would like to point out that Labour councils have environmental policies second to none throughout the country and have been responsible for a number of very successful green site policies. I would further like to make the point that not only is this Labour Party policy locally but also nationally. We are in fact the green party. With regard to this site *with unemployment being so high you have to weigh the environmental policy against the need for jobs.* Remember that in speech after speech the Labour Party and I in particular have demonstrated our positive policy on green issues and will continue to do so.

Q. As there are already twelve industrial sites in the area most of which are vacant why are you using green spaces?

R. As I have already said we are the green party and have a positive policy towards green sites. Which I would like to point out that neither the Conservative nor the Liberal Democrats have. The reason *an industrial site here would create jobs is that with the new road link directly to the M1 it would be very well utilised.*

120

Q. By building this site you will be destroying the area's main source of recreation. What are you going to do to replace that?

R. The Labour Party both nationally and locally have, as I have already said got a very positive policy on green issues. We are creating inner city parks and play areas faster than any of the Conservative led councils. In this case clearly things are under serious discussion and we hope to produce a consultative paper soon. Which can then be discussed at committee.

Q. So you have no plans to replace this green field site and local people will lose their only place of recreation.

R. *At the present we have no plans for this site.* However I am sure that if the Labour Party remain in power in the local area that eventually at some future date we will be able to provide an alternative to this site.

Q. So as for the foreseeable future the local community will lose its only green field site.

R. Yes that's right.

END So until the fourth and hopefully last public enquiry is held the fate of this beautiful parkland will be in doubt.

At last, the questions! Make them as short and as clear as possible. If the interviewee can't understand the question, there's not much hope for the answer. You may have a carefully thought-out order for your questions, but things never run according to plan. The interviewee might bring up a point in an answer that you had intended to keep for later, and it is easier and more natural to pick up the point and ask your question then. Don't be a slave to your question order; it will make you look as though you aren't listening to what is being said.

If you are doing a programme where you want to get someone's opinion, don't be afraid to phrase your questions in a way that leaves the person in no doubt as to what you want! 'What do you *really* think about that?' 'Be honest, do you really think it will work?' As long as you are polite you can be far more pushy than if you had met this person on a train. Remember you are the interviewer, it is your job, you have a right to ask detailed, probing questions and expect honest answers. You will be amazed how people will open up. Just think of what people like Jeremy Paxman get the stars to reveal on television! If you want to press someone on a point that is controversial, and you don't feel confident enough to meet them head on, you can always say 'But some people would think that view is wrong/dangerous/naive.'

Having got the questions and answers out the way, it is now time to make your life in the cutting room a lot easier. What you need to film are shots which can convincingly be used when you need to cut away from the interviewee speaking (because you have edited out a series of mmms and errs, for example) but which don't detract from what you will be listening to. The classic cut away, as they are called, is the 'noddy'. This is a shot taken from over the interviewee's shoulder (remembering not to cross the line – see chapter 10) of the interviewer listening intently and nodding (occasionally a laugh is thrown in too). This shot is best when the interviewee is talking so that she looks slightly animated (any talk will do as you cannot see their lips and you will not use the sound track – one favourite of news directors is to ask the interviewee what they had for breakfast!). Another of the common cut aways is the over-shoulder shot. This is really the reverse of the noddy: it is taken from over the interviewer's shoulder and shows the interviewer talking while the interviewee listens intently. This shot is often used as the interviewee is being introduced in voice over and so is sometimes called 'an establishing wide-shot'. Often the voice over introduction will lead straight into the interviewee's first answer and so it is useful if we believe (though we do not need to hear) that during this shot the interviewer is asking the first question. Consequently, some kind of talk is required. Another

122

Over the shoulder reverse shot (noddy).

Over the shoulder two-shot.

*Establishing wide
shot.*

common news trick is to explain what the shot is for
whilst it is being taken, this usually provokes the right
kind of nodding and frowning that is required of the
interviewee.

If you are making a film that involves contrasting two
different views or two opposing theories, a neat device
is to cross-cut interviews from the opposing camps.
This means that when you set up to film each interview
you should shoot one with the interviewee looking off
to the left of camera (i.e. get the interviewer to sit on
the left of the lens) and the other with the interviewer
looking the other way. If you have thought out your
questions carefully (and got each interviewee to repeat
the question in the first line of his or her answer) you
should be able to cut the interviews together – giving
the very clear impression of opposing arguments. This
cross-cutting works even better if the shot sizes of each
interviewee are similar, or if they have been lit to
contrast with each other.

124

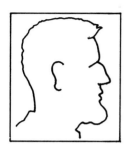

Councillor John
Herbert, for the
road.

Make a chart of
your subject's views:
those with a
particular viewpoint
are facing one way,
and those against the
other. Alternate
these on film if
possible.

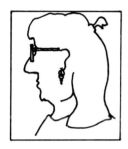

Mrs Pat Gill, Green
Party, against.

Mr Michael Parkin,
local business man,
for.

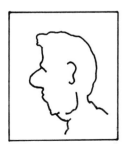

Mr John Newman,
local resident,
against.

125

Vox Pops

If your programme is about a particular issue or debate try to let the public have its say. The 'street' view can make a pleasant change from the official or politically interested view point.

To achieve this we turn to a technique called 'vox popping' which quite simply means 'the voice of the people'. Select a question or a couple of questions which are designed to stop people saying just yes or no. For example don't ask, 'Do you think Madonna's book should be banned?' most people will answer quite simply 'Yes' or 'No'. It is better to ask 'Why do you think Madonna's new book should be banned?' forcing them to give you a fuller answer. Also think of other ways of phrasing the questions just in case you are not getting the responses you want.

When you have decided on your questions get your crew together, explain to them what you want and hit the streets. Interview as many people as necessary to get all the replies you think you need. Make sure you have got a good cross-section of views. For certain subjects it is going to be important that you balance gender, age and in some cases race and religion (if, say, you were making a programme about racial harassment or *The Satanic Verses*).

Listen to the replies carefully and if you have the time make a brief note about who said what. Although you may not be able to use a person's whole answer bits of that answer can often be just what you want. Also try to keep the best or most humorous answer until last (it's normally the one your viewers will remember best). Also remember (as with most multi-interview programmes) to use the cross-cutting technique. For example, people who are in favour of Madonna's book could look camera right, those against camera left (and don't forget to leave some looking space). To have all the faces looking the same way can look very odd.

When vox popping a crowd try to focus in on one or two people, otherwise your camera operator is going to have problems following you and the whole thing will look a mess. Although vox popping will make a refreshing change to your film or programme don't let it take up too much room otherwise it will begin to be boring.

Pieces to Camera

This is probably the most direct way of getting information across to your audience; it is also the hardest. It is important that your presenter memorises his 'piece to camera': nothing looks worse than someone looking down at his notes all the time, especially if it is a vital or moving piece of information. If the presenter is struggling, try shortening the piece or make some cue cards and either hold them in front of him (out of shot) or stick them onto the bottom of the camera where they can be easily seen. You could also try cut aways or two shots to cover any joins in the commentary.

Unless the location is generally known or seen before the piece to camera your presenter will have to introduce it. To make this more interesting as your presenter introduces the scene you could either pan or zoom back from the scene to your presenter. Both techniques can look equally effective. As a piece to camera is normally done as a MS (Medium Shot) try to keep the mike out of shot. Use your sound man if you can or (if it is quiet enough) use the camera's microphone. There really is no need to have it in shot so avoid it.

Walking and Car Interviews

Try interviewing people on the move. Although slightly more difficult to do, mobile interviews can also be far more interesting than static ones.

127

Firstly, make sure you choose an area for your interviews that has smooth roads or paths, or you're lost before you begin. For a walking interview the camera operator has to walk backwards so try to ensure she has an assistant to guide her way. For a car interview the camera operator has the problem of trying to keep her shots steady despite the movement of the car. Although it is possible to buy car mounts (see chapter 4) if you haven't got one or can't afford one try improvising. A shopping trolley, wheel chair, or pram pushed along the side of the car can work very effectively. Also try to pick locations where the light isn't going to vary too much. Try to avoid woods or areas of road with a lot of overhanging trees and bushes.

For walking shots try to keep your subjects in a two shot, as medium shot (MS) or close-up (CU) can be difficult to hold steady. It's best to wait until they have stopped before trying those particular angles. When shooting a walking shot keep your subjects slightly to one side of the frame. If the subjects walk out of shot, make sure that they walk into the next shot from the opposite side of the frame or the whole sequence will look very bizarre indeed. Make sure that you get plenty of cut aways to cover any joins you want to make. It is possible that you won't even notice you have a problem at the time you shoot. It's only when you do the edit that it will raise its ugly head. With a good back-up of cut aways you can normally cover most mistakes. Get shots from the back, front and side of your subjects, shots of the area they are walking past or of the path or road they're walking along, points of interest that might be mentioned during the interview. Of course you won't use them all, but it is reassuring to know that you have got them.

For car interviews there are really only three shots: inside sitting on the front passenger seat shooting through the windscreen or across the driver, sitting in the front passenger's foot well shooting up towards the driver; or in the back seat shooting across the driver's shoulder or between the driver and passenger. From this position you can also get a number of good cut aways; driver's hand on the wheel, driver's hand changing gear, shots through both the back and side windows showing the car driving along, or, if you're feeling very arty, a shot of the rear view mirror giving the driver's view of what is happening behind the car (be careful however you don't get your camera in shot). It is also a good idea to get several shots of the car driving past your camera from a variety of angles. If you can afford it a car mount is also a good idea to get some outside shots of the car racing along and the wheels turning.

One warning: make sure you all have your seat belts on – you never know who might watch your film.

At A Glance

1   Preparation is vital. Don't think you can just walk in and wing it.

2   Consider the answers you want and think about ways of structuring your questions to get those answers.

3   Research is vital. There is no point interviewing someone if she quite simply doesn't know what you want.

4   Start with easy basic questions. Even if you don't intend to use them it will help your subject relax.

5   Think about your location. The pictures are just as important when interviewing as they are at any other time.

6   Try to interview your subject with a relevant backdrop e.g. a scientist in a laboratory.

7   Try to have an informal chat with your subject before the start of the interview. It may help you think of fresh questions and angles.

13

Graphics

Titles and Names

To add that professional finish to your programme it's a good idea to add titles. There are a number of points to consider when deciding what titles to use and where to put them. The layout and background you choose for your titles should reflect the type of programme you are trying to make. A film with a serious theme in a documentary style will probably require sharp impressive titles, while a comedy or 'holiday snaps' type content would be complemented by a relaxed or quirky style of title. Make sure your titles are legible, interesting and displayed long enough on the screen to allow people to read them fully.

It is possible to buy a camera with a built-in caption generator (see chapter 1). Your caption generator will enable you to add titles to your programme. These generators normally produce lettering of different sizes and colours which can be produced anywhere on the screen. The more sophisticated (and therefore expensive) generators will allow you to scroll your titles both up and down on your screen.

As well as creating your beginning and end credits, you can also use your generator to introduce additional information. A person's name, a change in both time and place, or an outline of where or what you are filming can all be indicated.

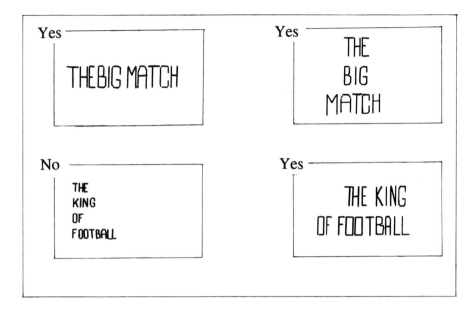

Do they look right?

Do not cramp your titles or stretch them to fit or they will look unnatural. Play about with your titles before using them and see if they work. Do they sit comfortably on the screen? Do they portray the right image for your programme? Are they interesting and attractive? One-line titles normally look best when they are placed in the centre of the screen. If you are using more than one line, make sure your titles are neatly aligned, normally to the right of your picture, positioning them about mid-screen.

If you don't have or can't afford a camera with a title generator you could try to create your own. It can be a lot more fun, and with a little imagination you can create far more original titles and layouts. Get a strong flat piece of board, which can be supported vertically in a fixed position on an easel or hung from a wall. Try using natural light wherever possible, but you may find you need some additional lighting. If you do

Do your captions sit comfortably on the screen and portray the image you want?

131

place lamps either side of your camera. Check your alignment and that your picture is centred correctly; any deviation will be very noticeable on the screen. Try a few shots and check the results before making your final recording.

Hand write your titles directly onto a light-coloured card (not white as that will produce too much glare). To produce clear, strong letters use thick felt-tip pens. You could also try using a paint brush, and do it 'Rolf Harris' style. Stencilling sets or transfer lettering are also very useful when you want to produce neat, even lettering. The sets are also available in a variety of styles and sizes and are readily available in most stationery shops.

When designing your lettering remember to allow for 10 per cent spacing all the way around the edge. This way you will not get any visual distortions when the titles appear on the screen. Don't mix the style of your lettering; it looks messy, can be illegible and will be extremely annoying to your viewers. Make sure your letters or lines are not too close together, otherwise they will look untidy and rushed. Deviations in lining up your letters will be magnified on the screen by an alarming amount. Pay attention to the spacing of your letters, making sure your distances are of equal width, thus giving your titles a well balanced and professional appearance.

The colour of your titles will depend largely on the cover on which you intend to lay them. As a rule of thumb avoid bright primary colours for a plain background. White lettering is probably the easiest to use for a neat, legible appearance. Backgrounds with a shiny finish could give you problems with reflections when filming. Keep your titles simple, bold and clean and make good use of the space you have.

These are only guidelines and there is nothing to stop you from trying effects which break these rules. If you are feeling very adventurous you could even try creating your own specially designed titles, using, say, marbles which role away and clear for the next title. Lights can also be used to produce illuminated names; by turning different lights on and off you can create the right patterns.

Make your own captions – it is far more fun and can look very interesting.

133

Rostrum

Rostrum camera techniques give you the ability to photograph static objects, such as newspapers, paintings, photographs and maps for inclusion in your programme, and will certainly give your film a polished look.

The set-up for using a rostrum camera is much the same as that for filming your own graphics and there are a number of points worth making. When filming, to help eliminate reflections from a shiny surface or a glazed photograph, tilt your camera slightly so its surface is not parallel to the camera. Before shooting try to work out the length of each shot. If you have some commentary about the shot try timing the shot to that (it's not a bad idea to overshoot just in case you change your mind about your commentary later). But if it's a shot of a newspaper headline or article try reading the words out loud and take your timing from that.

A basic rostrum set-up, including two lights, camera and a stable picture. Pick out the details you want, using movement if possible, i.e. zoom, pan and tilt.

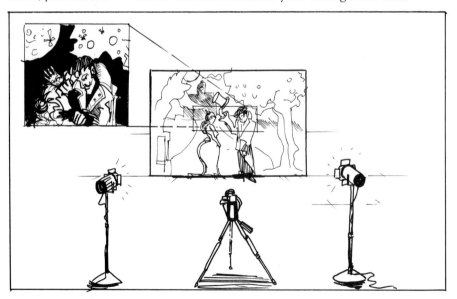

Often the object you are filming will be the wrong size for your frame. Don't worry, it doesn't really matter, and so long as the surroundings don't interfere with the shot it will look just as effective. Try wherever possible to introduce movement into your shot. It can make the static object you are filming look far more interesting. Try panning across a wide photograph or tilting down a long one. Remember to keep your camera movement smooth and even. Another interesting technique is to try zooming out from one particular area to reveal another or zooming in from a general view of a picture to pick out a particular section. You can also create emotion by picking out, say, eyes or zooming into them rapidly to demonstrate a particular feeling or emotion. With the correct commentary this can be highly effective. It is also possible to use a particular picture more than once by picking out different sections of it which might be relevant for different parts of your programme. So when you are filming a picture or a photograph try using a combination of these techniques; you never know which of them will come in useful later during the edit.

At A Glance

1   The layout and the background you choose for your titles should reflect the type of programme you are trying to make.

2   Although you can buy cameras with title generators try creating your own.

3   Remember to allow for 10 per cent spacing all the way around the edge to stop visual distortions when it appears on the screen.

4   Don't mix the style of your lettering or let them get too close together.

5   Keep your titles simple, bold and clean. Make good use of the space you have.

6   When using a rostrum camera make sure you get plenty of movement in the shots. Pans, tilts, and zooms can all look very effective.

14

The Edit

Put simply, editing is no more than the selection and arrangement of uncut material or 'rushes' into a finished or 'cut' film. In reality however it can be much more than that. Editing is both an art and a craft. It is a craft that you can learn by trial and error, or by example. It can also be very creative, and probably the best way to learn about film making. This is where you realise what you should have done when you were shooting!

Like every other area of film and television, editing has its own language and peculiar usage of words that is often historical and sometimes difficult to explain. But those terms are used in various forms throughout the industry and it is important that you understand the concept behind them.

There are several ways of editing, depending on the original material. For anything shot on tape, the material is dub edited. That means that the original material is retained and the shots you want to use are copied onto tape in the order that you want them. It's a bit like making your own audio cassette of favourite music tracks from different CDs or tapes. So if it all becomes a bit of a dog's dinner you can go back to the original and start again. For the simplest form of edit you use two machines. Shots are dubbed or copied from the rushes tape(s) in one video tape machine onto the cut story in the other machine. Exactly how you edit will depend very much on the equipment that you have. That will also determine the limitations on what you can easily achieve. The instruction manuals will tell you exactly how to effect a cut but the basic principles remain the same, whatever you are using.

Remember the only editing rule: there are no rules, only hints and tips. What is completely inappropriate for one production, say a drama, is fine when cutting a documentary. To apply any strict rule is to stifle any real creativity, so don't be afraid to try something if you think it might be a good idea.

Joining Shots

First let's look at a simple edit. The only real judge as to whether two shots should be joined depends in the end on whether they look right together. Watch television. Try to analyse why two shots work well together when you watch commercials, the news and even feature films. In news programmes lots of liberties are taken which documentary and feature film makers would howl at. These are dictated by speed or the nature of the story.

The Sequence

What distinguishes that from more planned and prepared filming are sequences. A sequence is a series of shots deliberately filmed to cut together to look like continuous action but all done with one camera. Take someone getting out of a car. You could have spent perhaps 10 minutes filming the action but in your finished film want the action to last just 30 seconds or a minute at most. Ideally the shots you would like to choose from would include the car pulling up from right to left and stopping when the door is in front of camera. The door opens in a medium close-up (MCU). The cameraman then moved around to the front of the car and you have a repeat action and another shot of the car arriving from the front view. Then a big close-up (BCU) of the passenger through the windscreen. The door opens from this angle too. Perhaps then the cameramen had moved back to the side of the car, and got a wide shot of the door opening and the passenger getting out. Now you could just use two shots to get your passenger out

A simply directed sequence which will allow the action to be cut together naturally.

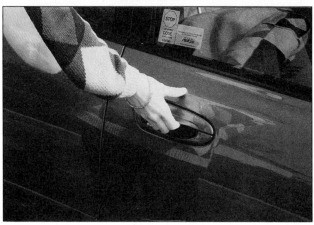

138

of the car but it will take forever and be somewhat dull. A close-up, say from the interior, of a hand going onto the door handle, another close-up from outside of a foot touching the ground and the door being shut, would liven up the action and more importantly save time for more exciting action. You may not have the luxury of this choice of shots; it depends if this sequence was directed or if you were lucky enough to have a highly competent cameraman.

Look at how film is edited to get the viewer from one sequence to another. Listen to how sound is used to help a join go through unnoticed or where necessary, do the opposite and help call your attention to the change of shot. Notice, above all, that in a well-edited piece, no edits are noticeable.

Let's say the film we are about to edit documents a race at an indoor swimming pool. The director has set up some shots, but some have had to be grabbed (shot quickly as it happens) by the camera operator. So although you have already decided what the film or programme will look like and what you want to say, there are still plenty of decisions to be made. The first sequence may well be a series of shots which build up the tension before the race starts. Imagine the first shot to be a wide, low angle, showing the pool in the fore-ground and the swimmers limbering up in the back-ground. Mark an in point on the edit machine (or recorder) where you want the film to start on the tape (probably about a minute or two into the beginning of the tape) and then mark an in point on the rushes machine at the point you think appropriate on the first shot. Remember it will take the viewer a little while to work out what the scene is, and you probably want to lead them in gently, so be generous and make the first shot 5 seconds or so at the very least. But don't stop where you think the first shot will finish. Lay it down much longer; you may change your mind about where the next shot should come in and you may well need the sound.

140

Now think about what you are looking at and notice whereabouts on the screen your attention is focused. It could well be on the swimmer in the blue swimming cap with her arms over her head. Look through the rushes for a tight shot of a blue cap either doing the same thing or the sort of thing that could reasonably follow it. Try to match the action on the two tapes by moving them both until you think you have a join that will work. Mark this point on the new or incoming shot as an in point on the player and on the old or outgoing shot as an out shot on the editor. Now think about the sound. You may feel that in order to make the join 'seamless', you don't lay any new synchronous or sync sound down from the incoming shot, but leave the sound from the outgoing shot. Rehearse the edit. If you don't like it, think about why it doesn't seem right and make the necessary adjustment. Otherwise record it. You've just made your first real edit.

Let's follow that shot with various others that help set up the atmosphere before the race starts. Perhaps another shot of a competitor (red cap) looking tense. A good trick here might be to come out of the tight blue cap shot when she looks 'camera right' (i.e. on your right as you look at the screen) to a similar shot of a red cap looking 'camera left'. You have already started to set a sense of competition – the two are eyeing each other before the start.

Now you plan to put some crowd and other shots in, then the shot of the starter. Here the most important aspect is the sound, the words he shouts rather than the picture of the starter himself. Let us assume you find that the starter was filmed after the race was finished as a separate shot, twice in fact. A medium close-up (MCU) shot of his head and shoulders first and then as a big close-up (BCU) of his mouth as he shouts out to the swimmers. Work out how much of the sound you want, let's say from the words 'on your marks' onwards. Lay the sound and pictures from the BCU until after the sound of the starter's pistol. Now you

141

can 'overlay' or edit over (vision only) some of that with shots of the swimmers, crowd shots and the MCU version of the starter saying 'on your marks'. Don't forget when editing in the middle of a sequence or inserting shots to also mark an out point on the editor, in this case before the starter says 'get set' on the shot that you have already laid down. If you were to over-lay the tight shot rather than the wider shot you may notice a discrepancy in, say, mouth movements. That's why we try laying down the tight version first. If it doesn't look right, change it, i.e. try editing in the sound as well over MCU starter shot.

Split Editing

Another technique you might try, if your equipment allows, is a 'split edit'. It means that the in point of the incoming vision is at a different point to the in point of the incoming sound. This is most commonly done in order to lead sound at a join. Let us imagine that the hero of this swimming race starts to think back to something tragic that happened the previous night. We have a tight shot of her swimming in the water already laid onto the edit tape. If we just cut to the terrible argument she had with her boyfriend it may not work, it may give us the impression that it is happening now, in another scene, and the viewer could end up very con-fused. To help the join, we may lead the sound 'under' the swimming shot by 5 seconds or so in order to imply that those sounds are going around in her head, then cut to vision. This technique is used widely and is usually very effective.

Adding Music

Try using music. In this case lay the music down first, then put the picture over that. Now the sound is going

142

to dictate where you edit as much as the action. You may consider using music that has the same pace as the swimming or you may like to try something that will contrast; it depends on the effect you are trying to achieve. It is important to realise the effect of the sound and the relevance of both sound and pictures together whenever you can. Sometimes sound will dictate what pictures are used and vice versa. Try cutting the pictures at different points in the music and see the effects. Often the most effective method is to cut a new shot at the beginning of a beat. But again, don't be afraid to try out new ideas. Sometimes it works well to cut on the off-beat. If the music is slow, you may feel inclined to exaggerate the action or drama of the race by using slow motion. Not all systems will have this facility, but it can be very effective.

Fading

Another very basic tool used in editing is the vision mix or fade. This and techniques like a fade down to black to another scene or a wipe of some sort become in effect the punctuation marks of the film. Again there are no rules, just think about why you might want to use any particular technique at any particular time. A mix might be used to move time on or it might be used to connect together various different scenes to gentle music. In order to mix or wipe, you generally need two 'play-in' machines. The equipment will dictate exactly how to achieve a mix or wipe and you will need some sort of vision mixer. You can then mix the shots by hand at the appropriate moment or rely on the equipment to do it for you. Again you must choose, but don't overdo the techniques (again assuming your equipment will allow) unless it seems appropriate.

The same guidelines should apply to editing as for directing (see chapter 10). Try not to 'cross the line' if you want to make sense of a sequence like the swimmer's flashback of the argument for instance. Consider using 'wildtrack'. This is sound, usually speech, that you can use 'wild' or anywhere, i.e. not synchronous with a relevant picture. This may be something that was recorded specially on location (sound only) or you may find your own from some of the sync (sound and vision together) material. You will put these onto the edited film by doing sound-only edits. If you want to space them out you may need to use 'buzztracks', that is the atmospheric sound on location, like distant traffic etc., to put in the gaps. This should help to make the sound track seamless. If when you have finished you don't like the finished product, you can always edit what you have already done onto another tape or 'go' down another generation. Put the edit tape in the player and edit from that onto another edit tape, making whatever changes you wish. You can add new sequences, and not transfer those that don't seem good enough. But beware. If you are editing on an ordinary tape system like VHS, each new generation will be degraded and look much worse that the previous one. This applies to a varying degree to almost all systems, so assess how many generations you can go according to the equipment you have and try to get it right first time.

Know Your Material

One of the methods that will help you to get it right first time is to know the material well before you start. If you can, look through all the rushes and log or write down a description of each shot or sequence next to the tape number (if there is more than one) and a time code. On some systems this may not be any more than a tape counter that you have to reset at the beginning of the tape. A much better system used by all professional equipment has a unique timecode for each frame which is recorded onto the tape at the same time as the

144

sound and vision. In this way you can accurately find shots and repeat edits to your heart's content.

Think laterally, be inventive: there are countless ways to edit something. None is right and none is wrong; some are just better than others and the very best edits can be wonderful. Above all try to enjoy editing. If you do, you're probably doing a good job.

At A Glance

1 Remember the only rule in editing is that there is none. There are only hints and tips. So don't be afraid to try something if you think it might work.

2 The only real judge as to whether two shots should be joined depends in the end on whether they look right together.

3 Get to know your material well before you start to edit. It can save you hours.

4 When looking through your material write down a brief description of each shot or sequence (with a tape number or time code if possible).

5 Watch as much TV as you can and see how different shots and sequences are cut together. It's the best way to learn.

15

Dubbing

Dubbing is a sometimes much misunderstood term used variously to describe the addition of effects and voice narration to a film, mixing of several different sound tracks down to one or two and generally finishing off anything to do with sound. This is usually the final part of any production and can sometimes transform what appears to be quite dull and rather ordinary looking sequences into realistic or even magical moments. Here I describe the dubbing process and how you edit sound with this in mind.

The use of dubbing comes from the traditional film industry. Originally shot without sound, or mute, the film sound would have been added or dubbed onto the film afterwards in large 'dubbing theatres'. Now, that same sort of process is used to enhance or even replace the sound obtained on location. You can use similar techniques with simple stereo video equipment. Although many modern video editing formats allow you to mix sound between different sound tracks as you go along, many do not and it is as well to understand the principles of dubbing as this may be the only way of obtaining a better and more polished sound track to your film.

How It's Done

When cutting 'real' film, editors have several sound tracks running at the same time as the pictures. They are not mixed as the edit proceeds but the sound is generally laid on alternate tracks with long overhangs both before the associated pictures and after it. Let us imagine we are cutting a sequence showing a man nervously walking through a wood. The first shot in the sequence could well be a wide 'tracking shot' taken from behind the man, with the camera effectively creeping up on him, followed by a much closer shot over the shoulder as he turns and is surprised by . . . a thing! The vision cut is made at the appropriate point but the sound from the first shot is laid (onto track A) much longer. This is usually until it can be of no more possible use or more likely until the shot ends and someone shouts 'cut' or similar. The sound associated with the next shot (the close-up) will be laid onto track B, but from a long way before the shot is actually used and as before, until a long time after the shot ends. The third shot in the sequence (a close-up of the thing that surprised him perhaps) would have its associated sound either on track A or, if the second shot is very short onto another, track C, using the same principles. There may also be music associated with this scene, and even a voice over, perhaps the voice of the man, recollecting from his hospital bed what happened to him. You know the sort of thing: 'I was feeling kinda nervous as I walked through them trees, I can tell you. All of a sudden . . .' Each of these sound sources would also be laid on a separate track, which in this example gives us 5 sound sources to mix down to 1 (or 2 if the end product is stereo).

It could well be that the sound on location may still not be good enough, in which case effects may be played in off audio disks, tapes or CDs, or even created in the theatre. Dubbing is also used to make foreign language

147

versions of a film or programme, and to over-dub bad singing, talking and even bad acting. All this is the art and craft of dubbing.

Mixing

The purpose of overhanging the sound joins is to give the 'dubbing mixer' many possibilities of getting the sound mix just right. It may well be that as the camera approaches the man in the first shot you may want to use the sound from the second shot, as the sound of half a dozen assorted technicians following the camera through the wood just doesn't create the right atmosphere. By the same token, it may sound just right – exactly like the 'thing' that surprised him in fact. Quite likely it will be a bit of both that will win the day with perhaps a crack (as the thing stands on and breaks a twig) added as an effect. The dubbing mixer may well play and mix a certain join like this again and again until it appears entirely believable and has the right dramatic or realistic feel intended by the director and editor.

Adapting Your Equipment

You can achieve something similar to a professional 'dub' on a variety of much simpler systems, by varying the techniques used in the dubbing theatre. Let us try to re-create the 'man-in-the-wood-gets-surprised-by-the-thing' sequence on simple stereo video equipment – a sound mixer and a sound 'booth'. Edit the sound onto two alternative stereo tracks as above, leaving an 'overhang' at the beginning and end of each shot. Create a sound booth in a separate room with a rather 'dead' atmosphere. Reduce sound reflections by hanging loose and heavy curtains around the room or, more permanently, fix foam pinnacles to the walls. Experiment with

the sound quality. Put in a desk, a chair and a microphone, read a script and listen to the sound quality
as it appears on tape. Add a 'cue' light if you can, a
simple lamp that you can operate from outside the
room. A monitor or television will also help, showing
the programme or film that is to be dubbed. Take care
not to put it too close to the microphone as this is often
the source of a high-pitched whistle. Seat the 'voice' –
the narrator, actor or reporter, depending on the type
of film or programme – comfortably, usually with a
glass of water. Put the edited tape with the alternate-
laid sound tracks into the play-in machine and a blank
tape in the recorder or edit machine. Set the recorder
running with its vision input from the play-in machine
and the sound inputs from the mixer. Run the play-in
machine and mix the sound as you wish onto one track
of the new edit tape. At the appropriate moment press
the 'cue lamp' button and mix the voice over onto the
finished article as well. If you as the mixer or the 'voice'
make a fluff, run back and do an edit before the point
where the mistake was made and try again. When
finished you can add music or effects where required
on the other track on the new edit tape. Play the two
finished tracks together and there you have it. Dubbing
magic even for the beginner.

*Don't sit too close
to the mike; this will
cause a high-pitched
whistle. Make
yourself comfortable
and speak slowly
and clearly.*

149

If your system is more sophisticated and you have a timecode available, play this into the booth somehow. If the equipment will allow, insert it into the image on the monitor in the booth and put the same numbers on to the script as 'cue times'. Alternatively, use a tape counter and re-set at the beginning of the film. If you cannot create a sound booth, you may be able to use a lip-mike – the sort of microphone that sports commentators use – in the same room as the equipment. That way you won't need things like a separate monitor, a cue lamp and several yards of curtaining. The 'voice' should be able to see the same monitor as everyone else and a little arm waving should suffice for 'cues'.

A good help may be a 'dubbing chart', a visual indication of what sound is on what track, and therefore on what sound fader, at what time. Write down on the chart the timecode or tape time at every shot change, every event and when each sound overhang starts and stops. If you don't, it will probably make as much sense as stirring porridge with a paper straw.

The disadvantage of taking the edit programme another generation is that the pictures and indeed the sound might actually get technically worse in an attempt to make it better. Try to know the limitations of your equipment, but don't let that limit your ideas or ingenuity at getting around those technical drawbacks.

When it comes to dubbing, be inventive, especially with effects. Go to the cinema and if you can bear to spoil a good film, don't listen to the plot, ignore the rustling crisp packets and listen to the sound track. Try to work out how much of the sound that you finally hear is anything like as it was recorded on location (probably very little) and imagine how the rest might have been created. Think about the role the sound track has in creating atmosphere, drama, suspense etc., and notice the effect that it seems to have on everyone around you. Then apply some of that to your own film. If something just doesn't seem good enough think hard about how it might sound better. Try adding effects

using everyday objects; the obvious ones like feet in a tray of gravel, doors shutting etc., the not so specific, such as atmosphere recording of birds singing in the woods, distant traffic. Perhaps you should re-create the sound of something like a crowd scene; record the sound using a few friends or colleagues by using a tape recorder or even a video camera. Then dub that over the film by editing it on spare track where you want it. Try simple music, nothing too strong.

Collect your own sound effects. You will find that even the quietest location, such as a church, has its own particular ambience.

151

At A Glance

1 Dubbing can transform a dull ordinary sequence into something realistic and impressive.

2 While watching TV and films see how the director uses the sound track and what effect it has in creating atmosphere, drama and suspense.

3 Try creating your own sound effects using everyday objects, such as feet in a tray of gravel, doors shutting or the old two halves of a coconut trick.

4 For the sounds you are unable to recreate get hold of some sound-effect discs and tapes. A good selection of music is also very helpful.

5 Create a dubbing chart as a visual indication of what sound is on what track. It will save you hours and help you organise your film.

6 When creating a sound booth for your narrator make sure that it's situated in a separate room from you with as little noise as possible. You can reduce sound reflections by hanging loose and heavy curtains around the room. It is also a good idea to add a cue light that can be operated from

Conclusion

Now that you have hopefully picked up a few of the basics you can start to produce your film. Don't go mad. Keep it simple and short, about ten minutes to start. Pick a subject you have an interest in. Practise the techniques and as time continues and you begin to learn your craft you will be able to make more complicated programmes. Anything will do, 'A day in the park', 'The weekend away' or perhaps a little more serious documentary, 'Save our pond' or 'No more car parks'.

Before starting make sure you have got all the equipment you need, and that it is working properly. Next try to work out what you want out of your film, and the best way to achieve that. A treatment or a storyboard will help. Make a few notes about what you want to say in the film and the kind of sequences, cut aways and sounds you will need to complete it; notes really do come in handy. Don't be scared to experiment and take as many shots as you think you will need. Those you don't use you can always tape over later. But most important of all, get to know your equipment. Learn how to use natural and additional lighting; the best way to use your zoom and wide-angle lenses, when and where to use your tripod, and how pans and tilts can best be used.

Most of all enjoy what you are doing. I did, which was one of the main reasons I finally made it my profession. I've only been able to scratch at the surface with this book so read other books and magazines. There are also a number of video courses you can go on which will help you to put into practice what you read in the books and learn in the class room. Watch as much good television as you can; the directors and producers who make these programmes have learned their art and can teach you a lot by example. So good luck and don't forget:

ENJOY IT!

Glossary

Accessory shoe A clip for attaching lighting or other accessories to camcorders.

Ambient noise The background noise at a location.

Aperture The amount of opening of a lens.

Audio dub The erasure of the original synchronised sound by the substitution of new sound.

Auto iris Auto control of the aperture of a lens.

Backlight Cause of under-exposure of the main subject due to light coming from behind.

BCU Big Close-Up.

Betamax Half-inch video cassette format. Obsolete in Europe.

BLC Backlight compensation.

Boom An extension arm for mounting microphones or the echoey quality of room acoustics.

Bounce light Illumination of your scene by reflected light.

Cardioid microphones Microphones with forward directional characteristics.

Camcorder One-piece combined video camera and recorder.

Clean edits Cutting or edit points to get rid of disturbance in the picture so no edits are visible.

Colour bars A video colour test signal formed by eight vertical bars – white, yellow, cyan, green, magenta, red, blue, black.

Colour temperature The colour quality of a light source.

Continuity Ensuring consistency of detail from shot to shot, i.e. eyeline, clothes, position of subjects etc.

Contrast The range of brightness from highlight to shadow in a picture.

Crabbing Moving sideways with camera, normally done with a dolly.

CU Close-Up.

Cue/review Forward or reverse picture search of a video tape.

Cut away Pictures taken to cover your main shot or interview. They are also good for hiding mistakes and jump cuts.

Cut on action A cut which carries a continuous action over from one shot to the next.

Depth of field The range of distances within a shot which are in sharp focus.

Diffuser Filter for softening the effect of direct lighting.

Dolby Noise reduction system for audio recording.

Dubbing The copying of a recording onto another tape.

Dynamic microphone A microphone which works on the moving-coil principle.

Edit-in camera The technique of shooting video in sequence order and length.

Effects Background noises for dubbing onto a recording.

Enhancer Sharpens outlines and edges of pictures and improves general picture definition.

Establishing shot Normally a wide or long shot which is used to open a sequence.

Eyeline The direction in which the subject is looking.

Fade in/out Increase or decrease in the brightness of the video picture from/to white or black.

Fill light Soft light to fill shadows produced by the main or key light.

Filter Transparent material used to change the colour or intensity of light.

Format Type of video tape you are using.

Frame Complete scan of video pictures.

Graphic equaliser Device for selective filtering of sound signals.

Gun microphone A microphone with a highly directional pick-up area.

Jog/shuttle The editing control dial found on a video edit machine.

Jump-cut An edit which interrupts the continuity of continuous action.

Key light The main light which provides the modelling for a subject and sets the exposure.

MS Medium Shot.

Noddies Cut-away shots of an interviewer's visual response.

Omnidirectional microphone A microphone which is equally sensitive to sound coming from all directions.

Pan Horizontal movement of the camera.

Pan head Device fixed to a tripod enabling the camera to be panned.

Photoflood Tungsten lamp used in photographic work.

Sequence Succession of shots in an orderly arrangement.

Shooting script Script which gives details of the camera angles action, etc.

Storyboard Series of rough drawings in preparation for a filmed sequence.

Telephoto lens Lens with a long focal length for magnifying distant subject.

Tie-clip microphone Small electronic microphone which attaches to your subject's tie, shirt, etc.

Tilt Rotation of the camera vertically.

Time code Electronic numbering of frames for accurate video editing.

Treatment Outline for your film or programme.

Two-shot Shot showing two people only.

Unidirectional microphone Microphone sensitive mainly to sounds coming from a single direction.

Voice over Part of an interviewee's speech heard over related pictures.

Vox pops Short informal interview of ordinary people's opinions on a subject, normally taken on the street.

White balance System for adjusting the colour balance on a camcorder.

Wind gag A sleeve placed over a microphone's head to prevent wind noise.

Wildtrack Unsynchronised source of sound effects for dubbing.

Zoom Lens of variable focal length. Bringing your subject closer or pulling back for a wide-angle shot.

Advisors

Nick Stuart
Nick Stuart began his career in 1983 as a radio reporter with Two Counties Radio in Bournemouth before becoming head of News and Sport at Southern Sound Radio in Brighton in 1986. In 1987 he moved to Thames Television where he worked as both a reporter and a presenter on the popular network series *Visions* and *Currents*. Since then he has been in continual demand as both a presenter and reporter, as well as being nominated for a number of prestigious television awards. Among his many successes have been, *Stories of the Month*, *A Time to Die*, *It's my Belief*, *Thames News* and more recently BBC 1's *Heart of the Matter*.

Richard Dale
After reading Natural Sciences at Christ's College, Cambridge, Richard joined the BBC in 1987. Winning a place on the BBC's elite 'Trainee Assistant Producer' programme, he worked in both the Documentary Department of the BBC and in news and current affairs.

He joined the Science and Features Documentary Department in 1989. He worked on the award-winning BBC 2 series *Horizon* and on the BBC 1 science flagship *Tomorrow's World*. In 1992 he became the youngest person to produce the programme in its 27-year history.

Richard is currently producing and directing programmes for the popular BBC 1 series *QED*.

Ian Lilley
Ian Lilley has been a cameraman, editor, director and producer since joining the BBC in 1979. He now works as a freelance producer working on both network and regional programmes. He has produced a wide variety of programmes, mainly current affairs and documentary including a 10-part topical series, nominated as the best news and current affairs programme at the British Environment and Media Awards, 1991.

Acknowledgements

Nick Ross, for finding the time to write the foreword and for his continued advice, friendship and help.

Jessop Camera & Video shops in Nottingham and Leicester, for the loan of their equipment.

Cathy Jessop, for her time, advice and help.

Paul Roper of Jessops Camera & Video shop, for reading the text and for his invaluable advice.

Peter Hiscocks, for giving me my first opportunity at film making.

Luke, Emily and Rebecca, for their modelling skills.

My wife Gill for reading the manuscript and modelling.

Jane, Matthew and Hannah Polkey, for their help.

Tim and Deb Culverhouse, models to the rich and famous.

Julia McCrery, for getting so close to a cow.

Ashley McCrery, for his help and assistance.

Kanu Patel, the man from the corner shop and super model.

Sian Parkhouse, my friend and editor.

Nick Webb at Simon & Schuster, for agreeing to publish this book.

Aruna Mathur, my designer, and all her friends and family.

James Smith, for his drawings and artwork.

Panasonic cameras.

Amanda Hepton-Patchett, because I spelt her name wrong in the last book.

Alan (the Bill) Clay, my friend and model.

Eric Handcock, one of the best cameramen and teachers around.

Fred Sturman, for teaching me about sound.

Hilary Cook, for teaching me the art of PA work.

David White, for his lessons on lighting.

Steve Clinch and Ken Murphy, for their hours of hard work trying to show me the art of editing.

All the people who have helped me over the last three years to understand the wonderful activity of film making.

Index